Tim McEvitt

Adventures of an Ordinary Monk

The search to make sense of it all

First published in paperback by
Michael Terence Publishing in 2025
www.mtp.agency

Copyright © 2025 Tim McEvitt

Tim McEvitt has asserted the right to be identified as
the author of this work in accordance with the
Copyright, Designs and Patents Act 1988

ISBN 9781800949843

No part of this publication may be reproduced, stored
in a retrieval system, or transmitted, in any form or
by any means, electronic, mechanical, photocopying,
recording or otherwise, without the prior
permission of the publisher

Quoted text from Bhagavad Gita As It Is,
Srimad Bhagavatam and Srila Prabhupada Lilamrita
courtesy of The Bhaktivedanta Book Trust International, Inc.
www.Krishna.com
Used with permission

Cover design
Michael Terence Publishing

Painting of Krishna as a boy
courtesy of The Bhaktivedanta Book Trust International, Inc.
www.Krishna.com
Used with permission

Photography
courtesy of Tim McEvitt and friends

Prologue	1
1 – 1993: The Beginnings	5
2 – 1994: Books are the Basis	33
3 – 1995: The Lake Isle of Inish Rath	53
4 – 1996: India, Hungary and Island Days	73
5 – 1997: Island Life	95
6 – 1998: Grace	111
7 – 1999: Y2K Preparation	129
8 – 2000: Learning to Love Together	143
9 – 2001: Dublin	153
10 – 2002: UCD	163
11 – 2003: Four Hungarian Girls	173
12 – 2004: Machine-Gun Chanting	187
Epilogue	197
Addendum	202
Thanks, Photo Descriptions and Credits	205
List of Well-known Sanskrit Words	207
Appendix Sankirtan	211

Prologue

In the East, two categories of monk are accepted and customary.

There is the older renunciant monk who is dedicated to spirituality and serving humanity. This monk will not marry.

And then there is the young student monk. He may have marriage, children, work and independence later on; but for the moment, he is in a stage of self development and preparation.

This is a story about a young student monk living on the Western edge of Eurasia – a student of an ancient tradition from India.

- Reading the ancient text, Srimad Bhagavatam -

- Young monks Shyamananda Das and Tim -

1

1993: The Beginnings

"Come out of the van, with your hands on your head," demanded a harsh voice with a thick Belfast accent. Spotlights were shining on us from all angles, and I glimpsed armed soldiers preparing for battle, racing to find cover behind trees and boulders in the fading light of dusk.

I had been reading peacefully in the front seat, and we had parked up in a remote hilly area of County Tyrone. As usual, we had planned to stay the night in the van, but parking it off the beaten track.

The three of us complied and slowly emerged, hands-on-head, blinking into the lights… it was just like a scene from an American action film. We stood in line as they frisked us, which seemed excessive as we only had light pyjamas on.

The RUC[1] and the British soldiers performed a thorough search of the van. "We're monks," we offered politely, although they weren't taking any chances.

"What the hell are these?" an army man demanded sternly, pointing at a suspicious clump with his rifle. "It's incense!" I responded innocently. In India, one can purchase a cylindrical clump of 300 incense sticks neatly bound up together. I suddenly realised that, in this scenario, these fragrant sticks could well be mistaken for new-design dynamite, or even exotic drugs.

---

[1] *The RUC (Royal Ulster Constabulary) was the police force in Northern Ireland between 1922 and 2001.*

We showed the soldiers our stock of books and started gently preaching to them – sure it seemed like the safest thing to do. Eventually, realising that we were not the IRA,[2] they released us. They didn't apologise for the inconvenience. We didn't expect anything anyway. This was the time of the Troubles, a time of unrest and violence in Northern Ireland between people who wanted to remain politically connected to Great Britain, and Irish people who wanted to break away from the United Kingdom. We were ordered to return to the nearest temple, which was in the neighbouring county. We had been travelling around the island of Ireland sleeping in the back of a van, selling Hare Krishna books for a pound or two on the streets of towns and cities.

I was 18. The year before I had been in school, and had managed 14 years in education without getting into trouble. How did I get here?

***

One day, a boy was lounging on the sofa, about to flick through the *Irish Times* when an advertisement on the front page caught his attention. His heart lit with fascination when his eyes met terms like 'Philosophy' and 'Eastern wisdom'. Within a few moments, his brain was digesting the signing-up details.

Northumberland Road is a leafy avenue with three-storey residences, originally the townhouses of 19th-century wealthy gentlemen and their families. The mature, roadside trees and fired-brick walls of the spacious houses exude a sense of period refinement and opulence. The boy ambled up old steps and gradually found his way to a seat in a tall-ceilinged conference room. At age 17, he was the youngest in a room of

---

[2] *The Provisional IRA (Irish Republican Army) was a paramilitary organisation active (for the most part) in Northern Ireland from the 1970s until the 1990s.*

adults born anytime between the 1930s and 1960s. The speaker at the philosophy talk mentioned that, just as the word 'Gúna' is a word in the Irish language for a dress, the Gunas (in the Sanskrit language) are dresses or coverings over the Self. Sattva is the mode of goodness, Rajas is passion, and Tamas is ignorance. "Someone who is an evil dictator is not intrinsically evil forever. However, at present, he's made choices such that he is now covered by mad passion and dark ignorance. If we choose the way of goodness, we will be happier. If we are sometimes not happy, the cause can often be traced back to choices or mind-patterns that we ourselves chose."

The speaker mentioned that this wisdom is coming from a book called 'Bhagavad Gita'.

"There is much to learn", thought the 17-year-old boy, and he yearned to learn more. That 17-year-old boy was me, a fresh-faced youth with strawberry-blonde hair, who liked reading, cycling, and quiet time

***

I was born in 1975. As youngsters, we read comics (and months later sold them to friends for one or two pence), played with marbles, got *Star Wars* figures and space-ships for Christmas, bought packets of crisps in local shops for 8p, climbed trees, kicked footballs, watched 'ET' - but just at Christmas time - and meandered around the housing estate with a brother or a friend on the back of a long-saddled bicycle.

When I was a boyish adolescent, my father (who always saw the benefit of travel to broaden the mind) brought us – my mother, me and my younger brother and sister – to the Black Forest region of Germany. One day, I worried them. I disappeared for hours into the forest on my own. I guess I had a desire for the tall, old trees to unveil their peace to me.

Nowadays people will go forest bathing as part of a holistic experience. So similarly, I guess I simply enjoyed and appreciated the profound calm and serenity of the woodlands.

I began First Science at University College Dublin in October 1992. During breaks and intervals I would visit the chaplaincy daily, which had a round meditation room that overlooked a Zen-like garden. The muted curved walls gave the space a striking full-bodied stillness. In a meditation book I came across the Prayer of St. Francis of Assisi, so I often repeated this slowly in my mind in the calm room. I was developing a desire to go deeper and discover myself.

***

One crisp Saturday afternoon at the beginning of 1993, I found myself aimlessly roaming around a different landscape – the brick-and-stone jungle of Dublin City Centre. Essentially, I was looking for happiness, but not knowing where to look, I wandered. On Dame Street, a shop window display caught my attention: ancient, Eastern. "Oh, look, there's that book, 'Bhagavad Gita'."

Beside the holy book there was a colourful sculpture of a cruel-looking Minotaur about to behead a terrified man who had the body of a bull. "Good Lord," I thought. To the left there was the Changing Bodies diorama: a sequence of sculptures depicting the circle of life and reincarnation - from embryo, to baby, to toddler, to boy, teen, young man, man growing in responsibility, mature man, old gentleman, ancient man collapsing, and finally to a skeleton. A light shone from the heart space and flashed between the embryo's heart and other stages of life all along its journey. Finally, the light flashed in the heart region of the body of bones, flickered out, and then started again in the embryo.

My interest was piqued as I entered this unique and intriguing place, and a bell tinkled along with the moving arc of the door. A gentle sense of awe and fascination washed over me as I pottered around this little shop of exotica. A blue-covered book with a colour image of a multi-armed god-entity triggered a memory of childhood cartoons. 'The Science of Self-Realisation'. It looked like something out of Sinbad or Aladdin.

I decided to make a purchase. At the counter a decent type of man, who had one of the accents from South-East England, taught me a few tips about the traditions and philosophy. He indicated that practising sage-level bhakti-yoga austerities was desirable, and shunning sense gratification was the way of the yogi and devotee. It sounded cool and calming to be a sage. I didn't really know what to make of all of this, but I was curious to find out more.

Then he cheerfully offered me some holy food from a bowl on the shop counter. A pure sensation of culinary bliss exploded in my mouth as the laddhu sweet (maha-prasad extra-holy food) melted internally, igniting my senses and consciousness. My mind flew back and forth between the contrasting perplexities of rejecting sense pleasure, to enjoying the senses like a celestial god.

"What's going on here?" I thought.

Regular attendees referred to the area to the rear of the shop as 'the temple', and I began coming often, a few times a week. I was interested in the philosophy and the food. Mouth-watering, plentiful vegetarian dishes captured my soul and my senses, but particularly the philosophy was a breath of fresh air: substantial, mature, comprehensive and refreshingly free of vague, impersonal mumbo jumbo.

Veda is the umbrella term to describe the original, age-old Sanskrit texts of India. As Veda covers millions of verses over multiple books and categories – and as we give the endings of plural words an 'S' in English – the term 'Vedas' is more common in this language. The Vedas are the literary backdrop of what Hinduism became, and which in turn influenced the later Buddhism. The terms 'Hinduism' and 'Buddhism' are words invented by people to vaguely designate particular faith systems. But someone can call himself a Hindu and when one hears his philosophy it sounds atheistic. Or someone else can call himself a Hindu and believe in God and heaven. This is because people can interpret some texts in different ways.

Marauding horseback raiders from Central Asia began pillaging incursions into India a millennium ago. They gradually referred to the people beyond the Sindhu River as 'Hindus'. When Buddha came to spread love, the people inspired by him were later referred to as Buddhists. I came to learn that when personalities like Buddha or Krishna were giving teachings, they were sharing with all of us. They were sharing with humanity.

Krishna is the speaker of 'Bhagavad Gita'. This text is as significant to Hindus as the Bible is to Christians. An American Hindu politician being sworn into office will generally choose the Gita to replace the Bible, such is its importance. But who is Krishna? There is a question.

One evening in March 1993, the senior monk at the Dublin Temple was giving a lecture. He referred to Krishna's mother, Yashoda (pronounced Yah' show' dah). This was puzzling. They were indicating or referring to this Krishna as being God, with a capital 'G', but how could God, by definition, have a mother?

I was still confused that evening, but over the coming months I was to hear that maintaining loving relationships is one of Krishna's primary interests. The understanding in the tradition is that Mother Yashoda has a desire to love Krishna in a motherly way, so Krishna reciprocates and acts as her son. In this way, they can both taste the bhakti, or deep loving connection.

According to how a devotee wants to love Krishna, Krishna allows Himself to appear in that form. (Yes, there is a capital 'H' there. It is a tradition and choice to capitalise the pronoun of God in the English language). "Oh no, that G_d word... here we go with religion" some might say. But perhaps, just maybe, a small number of people interested in religion are seeking some kind of truth; not to deny that both many cheaters and sentimentalists who delight in the imaginary have infiltrated into religious groups.

The text *Bhakti Rasamrita Sindhu* outlines five primary *rasas*, or ways of exchanging love:

1. **Shanta (neutral):** The devotee respects Krishna, but keeps a certain distance.

2. **Dasya (servant):** The devotee offers service to Krishna as a higher power.

3. **Sakhya (friendship):** The devotee interacts with Krishna as a friend.

4. **Vatsalya (parental love):** The devotee loves Krishna as a parent would love a child.

5. **Madhurya (romantic love):** The devotee shares an intimate, romantic bond with Krishna, characterized by deep, oceanic love

As a side note, madhurya-rasa (spiritual romance) was particularly challenging for British Christian missionaries to acknowledge in the 19th century. They assumed the 'Hindoos' were indulging in some kind of debauchery with this concept. One can't deny that some so-called 'Hindoos' then and now have been known to indulge in fakery or sentimental nonsense, so a discerning spiritual seeker must be continuously searching within him or herself to distinguish illusion from reality.

***

As a cultural tradition still rolling on from the 19th and 20th centuries, most Irish people would dutifully attend Mass every Sunday. Back in early 1993 our local church in Laurel Lodge, West Dublin, was a temporary prefabricated structure which had been factory-made with low-cost materials, while the brick, stained-glass, wood, and subtle, calming finishes of the permanent church were being completed that year. I went to Mass every Sunday. I'm grateful to these traditions as, even decades later, I see myself regularly attending the Sunday noon service – just in a temple now, rather than a church.

Concerned about my newfound interests, and in the style of a typical *Irish Mammy*, my mother arranged for me to attend a Catholic Youth Council retreat which took place in the Wicklow Mountains just outside of Dublin. A couple of weeks previously, she had enquired from the Catholic Cult Watch department about Hare Krishna, but they had assured her that "Hare Krishna is not one of the dangerous ones!" Knowing I was exploring the temple's foreign offerings, my mother was wondering if my spiritual inclinations could be, perhaps, geared towards something more familiar.

So it was that I found myself one Saturday evening, sitting around a wood fire in a mountain lodge, with a gathering of 15 young women attendees and two 30-something facilitators, discussing how we felt about the people who crucified Jesus.

I had never thought about it before. When I put my mind to it, I commented and shared with the group that I was angry. I mean, Jesus came to teach people about love and righteousness. He was disgusted with the rascals commercialising in the temple, and he drew attention to the hypocrisy of flawed people who wanted to stone to death a woman accused of adultery. And the outrageous response of the authorities was to torture and crucify Jesus. It was a disgrace.

On Sunday afternoon, I got a lift back to Dublin City Centre with some of the retreat attendees. Emerging from the vehicle, after verbally appreciating the Christian goodwill of the driver, I mentally plotted the pedestrian route straight to the temple on Dame Street.

The Hare Krishna Sunday Feast, sometimes called the Love Feast in the late 1960s, is a cultural sharing event where one can connect with one's inner hippie and share a meal with 50 or 60 strangers. A typical schedule goes something like this: walk into a cloud of Himalayan incense, be immersed in the sounds of tinkling bells and mantra chants, become enraptured by a dynamic speaker expounding on the intricacies of Vedic philosophy. Sway in time, or dance exuberantly to ethnic drum beats and, finally, tuck into a lavish, mouth-watering vegetarian feast.

That's on a good day. You might come on a day when no one lights incense, and the speaker is a bit boring... or worse: he speaks strongly about something controversial and manages to either offend or alienate many of the attendees. Or maybe one day there's no one who can play a drum-beat on time. But this day – on my descent from the Christian mountain retreat – was to be a good day.

After the lecture, the Head Monk requested everyone to stand for the final Kirtan (chant music). Accompanying the singing of the Hare Krishna mantra, this monk played a medium-large, handheld drum, whose beats gradually quickened and intensified. The temple room was packed with 60 or 70 people, practically cheek to cheek, but still some people found space to begin jumping up and down with reckless free-flowing abandon. I stood, rooted to the spot, observing the proceedings with a scholarly interest and in the cool light of science. Or, more likely, I simply wasn't emotionally free enough to take part.

And then something memorable happened. An old woman standing next to me also began jumping up and down. Wearing a brightly coloured, floral sari, and being Caucasian by birth, she appeared to be a member of this group, but the greyish white hair gave my 17-year-old self the impression of age-old maturity. I thought, "Wow, I didn't think old women were even capable of jumping!" In retrospect, she was probably aged 48 or 50 at that time, but grey hair and a few wrinkles seemed *old* to a teenager.

In March '93, I turned 18. Hearing that 108 was a sacred number for Hindus, Buddhists and Krishna followers, I decided to refrain from eating food for 108 hours, as a sponsored fast for charity. At this time, I was physically light and thin, with a low appetite, and I found it quite possible.

I plucked up the courage to address the physics class at the university one day. The lecturer, an English woman, was the only professor who used a microphone, so after class she kindly lent me the mike, and I mumbled and fumbled to ask everyone for sponsorship for the fast. Over the next few days, students would stop me in the corridors and give me a pound or two, and I collected £80.

I fasted over four days while staying at my dear Aunt Frances's house. She was kind, she always liked to look after me, and she herself had a low appetite with experience in religious fasting. I hadn't really decided who to help with the money. It was just that I had a desire to give back and help people, so days later I approached a random charity can collector in Dublin City Centre. She stood patiently while I plonked in pound coin after pound coin.

There was about £30 left, and I was developing an understanding that the temple's spiritual wisdom was also charity work, so one day I stood by the temple's donation box and was similarly popping in the Irish pounds, with their attractive, antlered-deer image.

The Head Monk happened to pass by, and I was struck by how deeply he appreciated the tiny offering. His concern was so sincere and genuine that I was touched to the heart. I assured him that I was not giving *all* of my money, but rather some donations from a modest charity collection. His name was Tribhuvanatha Das (pronounced Tree-bhoo-van-ath). Throughout this book I refer to him as being our Head Monk. He didn't describe himself as such. In fact, he really wasn't interested in institutional titles of any kind. His modus operandi was to quietly go about his business of serving Krishna, his spiritual master's mission and humanity.

In May 1993 I completed and passed my first-year exams but applied to take time off so I could join the temple. So, one morning in June, around 4.00am, I was to awaken for my first temple morning programme, and I had a profound sense of exhilaration. This was what I wanted to do with my life.

***

The contentment of connecting with the sacred erupted inside of me. Head Monk Tribhuvanatha, sang the Mangal-Arati morning prayers using an ancient oriental stringed instrument called a veena. Even a hardened atheist would experience a touch of spiritual joy on hearing the age-old traditional sounds. What we called the 'temple' in Dublin was really a temporary city centre 'preaching' outpost. It was a place of worship for just 3 years, before the rental costs became unmanageable for the modest income of the place. Temples of the International Society for Krishna Consciousness vary enormously from one to another.

Technically to be a real 'temple' there must be installed Deities, or forms of Radha and Krishna on the altar, or of other forms of Krishna. Radha is the feminine counterpart of Krishna. She is also known as Hara, which changes to 'Hah'ray' in the vocative tense. A temple will have pujari priests performing altar ceremonies without fail several times a day, 365 days a year. But the 'temple' in Dublin – although we used that word – was technically defined as a centre of the International Society for Krishna Consciousness (ISKCON). Such a centre does not house arca-vigraha forms of Krishna, or Deities, and the ancient ceremonies are not performed every single day. Once a week on Sundays there might be one arati ceremony, but conducted with fewer rules. For example, someone who is not formally initiated (a ceremony where the person agrees to follow strict vows) might do this one ceremony a week. In a centre there is more flexibility for the residents. For example, if the five residents stay up late to attend some public function somewhere, and end up going to bed after midnight, they are allowed to – there and then – just decide to all get up a bit later in the morning. In a proper temple, however, such leniency does not exist. The ancient ceremonies are performed daily always on time. The standard starting time is 4.30am. The punctuality is shockingly impressive by Irish or Indian standards, and would rival the legendary precision of Japanese trains.

So when I initially joined the 'temple' it was technically a preaching centre. However, it was to be later on that same year I'd go to live in my first *real* temple.

***

Early on in June my head was shaved by Monk Giri using a simple blade. With Hare Krishna monks, a small tuft of hair is left at the back close to the top of the head. This is called a sihka. It demonstrates that one is aspiring to be Brahminical, or priestly. There I was looking in the mirror at a very white and extremely smooth naked sphere. There were bloodied cuts and pockmarks everywhere. I wore a hat for weeks to try to hide the mess, and to adjust to the new me.

For several months, I helped with this or that, whether handing out leaflets on the street, or chopping vegetables in the temple. During this time, I attended the Trip to Tipp

Music Festival, also called Féile. Years later, I was to hear that my younger brother Alan - then only 15 – was also there. Emphasising the word Féile (pronounced Fay-La), he had given the impression to our mother of an innocent get-together of traditional Irish music when, in fact, tens of thousands of Irish teens were swimming in a sea of beer, mud and rock music.

I attended as part of the Hare Krishna contingent, and our mission was to give out thousands of plates of free, sanctified food and to share the Hare Krishna chanting. Our team of 20 volunteers had a marquee and multiple vehicles. At night, the cars and vans were arranged in a circular formation, kind of Wild-West style, creating a central private space that we used for early morning chanting on wooden beads. The protective formation gave some seclusion for the devotees when they did their individual meditations.

Even after the final performances on the main stages, we'd still be chanting in the marquee, and kids naturally gravitated in our direction, attracted by the drumming and clashing of cymbals. As the night wore on, boys bopping around wildly began to throw beer cans and glass bottles. At this point, the festival security and police requested Tribhuvanatha – drumming furiously like a warrior monk – to call it a night, and the boys and girls gradually calmed down and trickled out of the large tent, with a few converts still heartily chanting garbled versions of the Hare Krishna mantra as they eventually stumbled back to their own tents.

***

The Dublin centre functioned as a place to share Krishna consciousness with people in Ireland's capital. Devotees were passing through regularly, staying for one, two or five nights. Tribhuvanatha Das, who had founded this little temple, was frequently going back and forth between Dublin and England. He knew many devotees from around the world, and sometimes they would pass through to visit him and help a little in the sharing of Krishna consciousness with the general public.

***

Student monks (brahmacharis) are not supposed to chat to the girls. Of course, they are supposed to be respectful, but remain distant – very distant. This was sometimes a little difficult when the girls were floating around shyly, looking very lovely, with a meek and calm manner, dressed in traditional floral saris.

I was requested to bring one Hungarian girl to Dublin's central bus station one day, walking from the city temple. The streets of Dublin evolved gradually over a thousand years, so some challenged urban planning is in place. It's a little bit like if city planners held a pot of cooked spaghetti in one hand, threw it in the air, and what landed on the ground was the street plan. Like an ultra-conservative man from another era or culture – but also because of the crowded footpaths – I walked a few steps ahead of this girl the whole way. As the spaghetti streets twisted and turned, I regularly looked back to see she was still following me. It was a quick glance: her beautiful flowing sari and covered head shone out as being exotic, traditional, and religious in an attractive way. I hoped she wouldn't notice that I thought she looked amazing. However, in hindsight, teenage boys could hardly hide such thoughts. We didn't talk as we approached the bus station. It wasn't all due to the fact that I was a neophyte religious fanatic! I'm a little shy by nature and I'd been to an all-boys school, plus I thought the girl was dazzling in her bright sari; but her gentleness, beauty and humility were what I found most attractive. I gave monosyllabic instructions as to which direction she should go next. She entered the bus station, boarded the bus – her brightly coloured sari disappearing from sight – and departed… never to return to Ireland again.

In August, Tribhuvanatha suggested I attend a three-month training course in the large temple just outside of London. As I had no money for travel, Monk Giri suggested I go out to Grafton Street, a principal pedestrian shopping street in Dublin, and sell some little books about Krishna. And that's what I did, somehow collecting the £30 needed for the journey. I simply approached random strangers, showed them the books and invited them to make a little contribution for one. I don't know how I managed that.

I got the overnight bus and ferry from Dublin to London and arrived in the Soho Street temple on the day of a huge festival, Krishna Janmashtami. People were packed into the temple room, in the fashion of a Tokyo train at rush hour, but with cheerful anticipation. The Soho temple is situated in a standard previous-century London building (not too tall by Japanese or American city standards) located in the Soho district, an area known for clubs, bars, cafés and night-life. Soho Street runs into Oxford Street, the busiest shopping street in London and Europe, and on the other end it borders Chinatown.

***

After prayers and musical chanting, later that night I found somewhere to sleep. In those post-hippie days, there were no rules. Simply with my robes and sandals as currency, and carrying a sleeping bag and Japa wooden beads, I could stay overnight with no questions asked and no formalities. I just about found a space in a corridor to lie down for the night. By the late 1990s, one had to fill in application forms and request permission to stay in a temple, but in '93 there was a sense of freedom and informality.

The next day, I travelled out of the city to Bhaktivedanta Manor. George Harrison had discovered Krishna in the late 1960s while he was a member of The Beatles, probably the most successful and popular music band of the 20th century. In 1973, he donated a mock Tudor mansion house and estate to the ISKCON Krishna Society in London. Through the 1980s, the local devotees had gradually improved their management of the facility. By 1993, the place was quite impressive.

Arriving at the Manor was a surreal experience. In the distance, I could hear an ecstatic Kirtan chant music session in progress. However, there was not a soul in sight, neither around the grounds of the house, nor in the long, dark-wood corridor which approached the Temple. Hearing but not seeing people gave the impression of a place that was both empty and alive… with a living, breathing, transcendent bliss woven into the very fabric of the structure. My heartbeat quickened as I followed the sound of the chanting. Breaking into a run, I couldn't help but wonder: where was everyone? Then, on entering the temple room, I saw a sea of devotees moving backwards and forwards in unison, their voices and minds filled with the loud chanting of the holy names.

The lead singer, Kripamoya Das, was intensely personable and engaging as he lovingly encouraged others to sing, chant and dance. He led a round of *"Hare Krishna, Hare Krishna, Krishna Krishna, Hare Hare. Hare Rama, Hare Rama, Rama Rama, Hare Hare,"* and everyone responded. Then, every now and again, he invited others to lead the chant for a round. Time passed, time stood still, and then time was forgotten about, as everyone was immersed in the moment.

Although up until this time, I hadn't personally danced in a kirtan, on this morning I was swept along by the crowd, and I followed in this joyful union of souls.

I'm grateful for my stay at Bhaktivedanta Manor, learning the culture and philosophy of Krishna consciousness. There were 20 attendees from around Europe on the course when I was there. Our day started at 4:00am, and the morning programme featured congregational chant music (kirtan), Japa – this is repeating the Hare Krishna mantra on traditional wooden beads – and a philosophy lecture. Later on, we swept the floors, and chopped vegetables for either the temple lunch or the Hare Krishna Food for Life (feeding homeless people). We also attended specific classes just for students on our training course. In the temple practical tasks are referred to as 'services'. As most temples don't have people employed doing cleaning, cooking, gardening and light handyman jobs, these services are often done by new recruits or residents. A typical day in a major temple is regulated as follows:

2.30am to 3.00am	Some more enthusiastic residents arise earlier than required. I did this myself, at times. Or, I suppose I could say, I sometimes went through *phases* of extra enthusiasm for meditation.
4.00am	By this time, residents are expected to be up. Men and women are in separate parts of the building. Everyone has a shower. Public nudity does not happen – even among people of the same sex, one is covered with a gumsha (a light cotton towel) around one's waist.
4.30am	Everyone gathers in the temple room. There are some traditional purpose-built temples in the world with domes and Vedic architecture, but the majority of temples – especially outside of India – are simply large houses. The biggest room in the house is converted to the temple room, and then decorated to appear exotic, Eastern and full with Krishna-related imagery.
5.00am	Readings, prayers and announcements.
5.15am	Japa. Personal meditation with the repetition of mantra on traditional wooden beads.

7.00am	The Greeting of the Deities. A five-minute meditation where music arranged by George Harrison is played from a CD or other machine. The main singer was Yamuna Devi Dasi. (As an aside, George had offered to help make her rich and famous with her singing in the early '70s, but she declined. She had a deep emotive voice which was full of presence, maturity and soul). After listening to the CD for a few minutes, the residents sing songs and mantras.
7.30am	Srimad Bhagavatam lecture – a talk and discussion on one verse of this 18,000-verse text.
8.30am	Breakfast.
9.30am	Services. Everyone does whatever practical activities they can do to help others or assist the temple with its mission: arranging events, answering the phone, washing windows, cooking, gardening, growing vegetables, painting, distributing literature to members of the general public, chanting the mantra on public streets, conducting ancient ceremonies, reading, writing, looking after temple visitors, chopping firewood, cleaning, managing, office work, etc. Often, tired residents would have a late morning nap after being up by 4.00am.
1.00pm	Communal lunch.
2.00pm	Everyone resumes service.
9.00pm	Bedtime.

As for free time, this varies from temple to temple. In my experience, we were always busy, but not so intensely that we felt over-worked. We had time here and there for personal reading or japa meditation, or relaxing and chatting. So this is a typical day in a temple ashram.

***

What is it like to transition from having one's own private bedroom in a modern suburban house, to moving into a communal ashram? In this new setting one might have to tolerate another young man going to bed much later, or someone might be fumbling around looking for some socks in a plastic bag at 3.00am. In my case, it was an adventure. People often would go to bed around about the same time, and arise around the same time. However, I quickly realised the benefits of using earplugs, added to which I would lie on my back and cover my eyes with a tee-shirt folded into a long shape to avoid being disturbed

It's generally observed that ashram living with others is easier for 18- to 25-year-olds, i.e. younger people. When older people join ashrams they are more stuck in their ways, and find it much harder to adjust. Older people living in temples practically always want their own bedroom. Things also tend to go more smoothly if the young person has little or no money. Older people and / or richer people tend to have less tolerance for ashram life. When the little room-sharing challenges come up, they start to think "Oh God, I need my own place. I want SPACE!" And with the financial means to do so, they can simply decide to leave and rent an apartment or house. A penniless person, on the other hand, has no such luxury. For them, there's no easy escape, and so they stay (hopefully), learning patience and resilience along the way.

***

Every Saturday evening we got dressed up and enjoyed a night out in London City Centre. We went *outside* the pubs, clubs and places of entertainment and had a great time. We wore robes or saris, with the mark of tilak on our foreheads, and we chanted and danced around Oxford Street, Piccadilly Circus, Leicester Square and Covent Garden. There was usually around 60 to 70 devotees chanting, accompanied by three or four dynamic drum players and seven or eight players of clashing cymbals.

It was always a pleasure when strangers would join in with the Harinam (pronounced Ha'ree'naam, said with the syllables flowing quickly together and with the final syllable rhyming with 'calm'). The 'naam' here refers to the holy names of Krishna. Harinam is a public sharing event which recognises that, as many of us don't have time to go on pilgrimage to holy places nowadays, the Harinam brings the holy place to us.

One morning I had a service to sweep the dining room after the communal breakfast where around 150 people had eaten. I glanced out the window and saw one saffron-robed young English monk pacing up and down murmuring on his personal wooden beads, quietly repeating the Hare Krishna mantra to himself. "Huh, look at him", I thought. "Does he not have any *service* to do?" I was thinking that doing something physical was *real* work. I was somehow proud I was doing *real* work, whereas someone else was loitering around… or, at least, this was the thought in my mind. We come to live at an ashram with an ego, and that ego needs some time to be trained. Or, we need to learn our place, and that our mission in life is to serve others in our own unique way. But we often commence the journey with immature, child-like conceptions.

Three months passed and the course ended. "It's time to come home, Tim," said Tribhuvanatha on the phone, calling from Dublin. "You know," I replied, "I think I'd like to stay," and in a very gentle, freedom-loving yet grave voice, Tribhuvanatha indicated I could do whatever I wanted. Then he said, "But, we need you here, Tim."

The next day I was on the bus back to Dublin, so I left aside the delicious gourmet meals of the Manor, the fancy facilities and hot radiators that came on at 3.00am, to be back with my sleeping bag and camping mat on the cold, concrete floors of the basement of the Dublin temple. It was December 1st, the start of the Christmas marathon. I will now explain about Srila Prabhupada (the final 'a' here is generally not pronounced, so I will omit it), book distribution, and the Christmas marathon. Distributing the holy books is said to be a type of san-kirtan, as the literature encourages and provides the basis for chanting the Krishna mantras.

The Story of Srila Pra'bhu'pad

Born in 1896, in Calcutta (now Kolkata), India, Srila Prabhupad (the middle syllable 'bhu' rhymes with words like 'glue' or 'too') was the founder of ISKCON, the Hare Krishna Society. Vaishnavism had been around for millennia, but Srila Prabhupad's unique contribution was to package one denomination of Vaishnavism in a way that allowed people from other cultures to embrace Gaudiya Vaishnava theology and traditions. So, one can find a Krishna person from many diverse backgrounds such as a Swedish humanist college professor, a Kenyan farmer, a Japanese dancer or a Brazilian car mechanic.

As a boy in British-controlled India, Srila Prabhupad was educated in the conservative Scottish Churches College and he accepted Gandhi's suggestion of refusing to accept the degree even after passing the exams. As an intelligent young man he found work, regardless, and later started his own business. As was the custom of the time, he had an early arranged marriage. However, his real interest in life was to find a way to share India's timeless Vedic wisdom outside of the subcontinent. This mission had been fostered and encouraged by his own father throughout his life, and by his spiritual master from the age of 26.

In India, it has been a tradition for centuries for spiritually inclined older people to enter – or return to – the monastic life. If one or both partners in a marriage are spiritually inclined they can amicably separate. This would not be considered the same as modern divorce, but rather the idea is that for a higher cause spiritual people are allowed to pursue their inclinations after their children have grown-up.

More commonly in history, it would be a question of men entering the ashram, and women going to live with one of their children. However this was not always the case, as all-women ashrams existed too, and it could well be that the wife was more spiritually inclined.

So, at the age of 56, Prabhupad gave up the comforts of home and the financial security of his business to dedicate his life to the mission of sharing Krishna consciousness and Vedic philosophy with the greater world. In this instance, his wife didn't share his enthusiasm or interest in pursuing a spiritual life.

***

After a 13-year period of preparation he boarded a cargo ship bound for New York. Disembarking more than a month later, having turned 70 *en route*, he entered the primary metropolis of the Western World dressed in saffron robes and with the mark of tilak on his forehead. Walking with head held high he strolled courageously into Tompkins Square Park, took out some small, brass hand-cymbals and then began chanting Hare Krishna. He played the simple metal instrument vigorously and emphatically. Gradually, a crowd formed around him, and people began making enquiries. Those people, mostly in their early 20s, began to gather around him regularly, and before long they had rented a small, storefront 'temple'. Their numbers increased and, within 12 years, there were 108 temples around the world.

Amazingly, just after Srila Prabhupad was born in 1896, a Vedic astrologer had made a prediction that he would cross the ocean at an advanced age and open 108 temples. This was in a time when swamis practically never left India: they were averse to what they believed to be the unclean association of foreign meat-eaters. Recognizing the limits of his time on Earth, Prabhupad emphasized that his teachings would endure through his books. He translated and wrote commentaries on many primary Vedic texts, ensuring they were accessible to any interested people into the future.

Book Distribution

'Bhagavad Gita' has sometimes been described as the Hindu Bible. It's a conversation between Lord Krishna and the warrior Arjuna, and is one of the two primary original texts on yoga, the other being the later 'Yoga Sutras of Patanjali'.

Srila Prabhupad translated and wrote a commentary for the Gita. Other texts he helped to present were the 18,000-verse Srimad Bhagavatam (Bhagavata Purana) and the Isha Upanishad. He also translated the esoteric treatise of the love of God, called the 'Chaitanya Charitamrita'. Additionally, there were many supplementary books, debates, recorded conversations and commentaries. But, apart from a few hundred Sanskrit scholars, theologians and philosophers, and followers of this religion, who on earth would buy and read these books?

***

From the late 1960s and into the early 1970s devotees of Krishna gradually discovered that approaching people directly, either in their own homes or on a city street, was the most effective way of distributing the books.

From the book *Srila Prabhupada Lilamrita 'Let There Be a Temple'*, Chapter 4.

"Back in 1968 when 10,000 copies of 'Teachings of Lord Chaitanya' had arrived at the temple in New York, one swami had wondered how they would ever distribute so many hardbound books on the lofty philosophy of Lord Chaitanya, but in 1970, with the publication of another book, 'Krishna, the Supreme Personality of Godhead', some of the devotees in San Francisco had begun going door to door, person to person, and sell the books. And not only one or two books but 20, 30, even 40 a day.

The enthusiasm was such that devotees in other temples had begun to sell increasing numbers of Srila Prabhupad's books. With the increase in book sales, the young men had begun travelling in vans, going out all day, day after day."

It had been discovered that by approaching an individual person on a city street, or by encountering someone at an airport or workplace, one could easily relate or align the themes of the ancient text to a person's interests, work, or personal challenges in life, and accordingly sell the books in this way.

The Christmas Marathon

In the early 1970s the new devotees of Krishna in North America discovered by accident – and collectively – that, as shops and department stores opened late into the evening in the weeks leading up to Christmas Day, they could stay out later and join in with the festive mood of the season, distributing more literature than ever before. This naturally evolved into the Christmas marathon – a competition to see who could sell the most books. Now, in terms of the Modes of Nature, goodness, passion and ignorance; a competition like this would appear to be more in passion – and out of step with the expectation that monks would practice goodness (sattva). However, passion is better than ignorance, or lethargy, so a little passion in selling spiritual literature was seen as something to be encouraged.

***

Over December 1993, I took part in the Christmas competition in Dublin. I sold around 25 or 30 paperback books daily, along with three to five larger books. I'm aware that in the history of religious cults or pyramid sellers, many people have been talked into selling something, with the main beneficiary being some money-making mastermind. In my own experience, a small paper-back book had what was called a BBT (Bhaktivedanta Book Trust) price of 60 pence. 30p per book was the printing cost for 100,000 copies bound for English speaking countries; 30 pence of the 60 pence was put aside to build major temples in India. An average donation might be £1.50, so 90 pence was left over towards shipping the books here from England or Sweden, the running costs of our local centre, or to go towards the Food For Life project in Dublin which fed homeless people. At least in my particular case, we were not bringing in a huge amount of money, and the income was not siphoned off for some clever mastermind's luxurious lifestyle. Rather the Head Monk was humble, austere, hard-working, selfless and dedicated. All Krishna temples are independent. There have been a few instances over the years where donations were misspent by some insincere leader. It can happen. It depends on the misunderstandings and impure motivations of certain people; common weaknesses of human frailty.

***

Since 1968, there have been millions of interactions between Krishna volunteers and members of the public in shops, airports, city streets, or just by going from door to door. Some encounters have annoyed people, while others have been deeply helped. Such is the nature of outreach: it may not resonate with everyone, but for some, it can leave a lasting, positive impact.

***

I remember one incident from that December. I decided to speak up at the time because I felt something was a bit strange. It was a precaution; possibly over-cautious. **I relate this story to show how well the Head Monk handled it.** I was 18 at the time, but could easily have passed as a 12- or 13-year-old. An older man visiting from another north European country did something a bit strange and inappropriate towards me in the shower room. I didn't mind that much, as I was a young adult and I could handle it, plus in my situation it was a relatively minor incident. However, I also noticed when we were doing book distribution on public streets he would often talk to, or 'preach to', young people who were just old enough to wander the streets without parental supervision.

Out of concern, just in case this man had a tendency to act inappropriately towards minors, I decided to mention something to the Head Monk, Tribhuvanatha Das. Our Head Monk took this very seriously and talked privately to this man, who was informed that he was under surveillance in relation to his interactions with children and teenagers. I might have been over-cautious. But I chose to follow my gut feeling just in case.

I feel the situation was handled as well as it could have been. My heart goes out to all the young people in both religious and secular institutions who didn't have the good fortune of vigilant and caring management.

- Radhadesh Temple in Belgium -

- Sharma Das on book distribution -

2

1994: Books are the Basis

I was privileged to spend the year of 1994 adventuring around the island of Ireland, distributing spiritual literature and discovering a little austerity. It's good for young men to experience military-like discipline... to some extent. Instead of bullets, our ammunition was spiritual literature. This literature aspires to awaken sleeping souls to the urgency of birth, disease, old age, death, rebirth and our ultimate function. Or that's how we saw it.

In the early days, we tend to think of ourselves as preachers and teachers, and people everywhere need to hear the message. Over time, however, the experience and the blessings of people help us to discover and see that we are just as much students as everyone else. One day it dawns on the preacher that he himself is a spiritual infant who really needs time to mentally assimilate the wisdom presented to him.

At times we stayed in a house by the kindness of others but, for the most part, we travelled around the country sleeping in the back of a commercial van. Later on there were more fancy facilities, like a third-hand camper van; but my first experience of travelling for Sankirtan book distribution was sleeping on top of makeshift wooden storage spaces over boxes of books in the back of a windowless white van.

'We' were parties of three young men, and in '94 and '95 there were three groups driving from town to town, whether it was Newry, Tullamore, Galway, Cork, Belfast, Killarney or Tipperary. We visited every town in the country.

I remember various incidents. A brahmachari, or young student monk, doesn't wear underpants or boxer shorts, but instead wears kaupins, which are basically what a sumo wrestler wears: two long pieces of cotton, one wrapped around the waist and the other goes over the first length at the front, and then is tucked down between the legs, under the groin area, and comes back up getting tucked into the waist chord. A brahmachari monk keeps two sets, washing one daily and wearing the other, alternating them for the next day. In the damp Irish climate and living in the back of a van there were times when Monk Peter from Lisburn still had wet kaupins in the early morning so he had a habit of warming them up and drying them over the flame of the gas camping stove.

At around 5.00am one dark, cloudless morning, Monk Derek and I were pacing around outdoors, murmuring our Krishna mantras on traditional wooden beads. The van was parked up in a remote rural area. Suddenly, the back door of the van was flung open, and out of it was thrown a spherical, burning ball of flames.

We stood motionless, open-mouthed, transfixed on the flying beautiful red-orange fireball lighting up the cool black sky. Our mantras paused, we both simply stood there for some time staring in wonder at the attractive warming light, like a candle in a dark stone church, or maybe it reminded us of a happy family experience outdoors at Halloween. Whatever it was, we were mesmerised for a while.

Peter's kaupins were no more. They had returned from whence they came – back to the elements of fire, air and earth.

***

Monk Derek met a young Californian seeker called Randy in a car-park during book distribution. They chatted and later spent an hour reading one of the books there and then. Randy went to stay at the temple and joined up. It was not long before he had joined us helping to share the books with the public. One day, Randy and I were driving around the country in a van. Small towns and villages can be challenging. They have too little footfall on the streets - you can stand there all day and not meet many people. Also they don't allow for the element of surprise like in a city. In a city there is noise and bustle everywhere and one can sneak up on an unsuspecting lost soul who requires saving (I'm not being serious here).

Irish villages can lack the excitement and interaction available in a city. We discovered that the best way to reach people was to walk from shop to shop, and chat to the owners or shop assistants in each business, café or pub. Randy would walk the village in one direction, while I went in the opposite direction. Eventually we would meet in the middle. However many country people here can be quiet and unassuming. Randy, on the other hand, was loud and excessively enthusiastic. One day I went into a little café and saw as he approached a man, extending him a warm happy clap on his back. The expressions on the faces of the village people in the café were memorable. In disbelief and gentle shock, it appeared to them like Hollywood had landed in their sleepy little settlement. Randy had Italian-like flamboyance mixed with American grandiosity and hippie idealism. Villagers stood open-mouthed as they listened to Randy's vibrant appeal.

"Hey guys. You're all looking great today. We have some amazing books here about wisdom, yoga and happiness. Take one with you. We ask for a small donation to cover the printing costs." People dipped into their pockets for pound coins, looking a little overwhelmed, but on the level of the soul I'm sure they were joyful. Surely.

***

A Vedic brahmachari or Krishna monk's first activity of the day is to murmur mantras of gratitude to the spiritual elders, and then promptly wash teeth and have a full shower. In the van, our shower consisted of taking a bucket of water outside, scooping up some water into a jug, and throwing / pouring it over ourselves to have a wash.

One morning, we had parked up in a coastal area along the Wild Atlantic Way. I remember trying to have a bucket shower in a deep, dark, deadly gale, the winds howling, the water flowing sideways out of my jug. The winds were so violent that I had to wrestle with the van door as it was being smashed back and forth. One monk recounted to me of an occasion when in the 1980s one of these groups of book distributors had a van door ripped off violently in a storm. It was then dragged along the road and hurtled off a cliff, so they had to return to the temple with a door-less van.

***

Within my own experience of the howling winds, there was something which provided a stark contrast. We had a music tape player which had a function that when it played to the end, it rewound and started again. We played a tape of Srila Prabhupad singing on the topic of Prema-Bhakti, or pure love. He had the deep, raw soul voice of an old man who sang from the heart; not an opera, pop or Bollywood singing voice, but one that nonetheless painted a picture of the spiritual world through sacred sound. The music was eternally comforting. When I woke up, and before the others were awake, I would lie in the back of the van in the pitch black, with furious gusts of wind roaring outdoors. I was cocooned in a sleeping bag… and listening to the holy monk singing on the tape player was a very simple pleasure in life.

***

In early '94, The Troubles were still an on-going concern in Northern Ireland. Planting bombs in public places was a tactic of the IRA, and sometimes of other paramilitary groups that opposed them. One day in Derry I left a box of 50 books under a bench of a pedestrian street. My back was turned away from the books for a few minutes while engaged in a conversation about Krishna teachings with a passer-by. I glanced back towards the box, only to see army and police personnel manoeuvring towards it, talking furiously on walkie-talkies and about to call in the bomb robot! I inched towards them, trying to determine from body language who was likely to be the least trigger happy. Picking my man, I got closer and called out to him.

"Excuse me. These are my books. We're monks."

We got into a conversation, and with their permission I went to the box, opened it, and showed them the books. The word 'religion' is not massively popular nowadays, probably due to abuses and deviations by so-called religious people over the centuries, which came to light in the 1990s. However, in this situation – to emphasise we're not militant *and* we're not commercial – I mentioned and emphasised the terms 'monastery', 'religion', 'monks' and 'sharing ancient wisdom'. The police and the army dispersed, allowing me to carry on with the preaching work on the street.

***

The ultimate and end goal of Bhagavad Gita and corollary texts is love of God, Prema-Bhakti. Krishna is a name of God. In the Vedic understanding, there is one God, just like the sun is the same sun, whether one is in Dallas, Copenhagen, Nairobi, or Tokyo. Whether one calls the sun *an ghrian* (in Irish), sol, or surya (Sanskrit), everyone knows it is the same sun.

But we can see the sun. We can't see a God, so how can we know whether He or She exists? Well, there are a lot of things we can't see. We can't see microwaves, radio waves or X-rays. Unless we have personally been to Timbuktu, we might question if it ever existed. However, we naturally have faith in certain things, even when we can't see them.

So, we can't see God? Maybe we can. My understanding is that in order to see God, we need to be aware of who we are looking for. If God exists, is He or She a person, an energy, or both? Some 'evidence' may be all around us. My own body can be compared to a machine – a very complex machine. In terms of structure, my body is so much more complex than my computer or my car. Did Nature make my computer on her own? No. Intelligent human beings excavated the earth in search of various metals and petroleum. In turn, petroleum-based plastics were fabricated, and these raw products were assembled into complex machines.

If we look on Nature as a blind impersonal energy where atoms simply bounce off each other randomly, could this Nature have assembled my computer on her own? No. Creating complex systems requires an intelligent being or beings. Do I know who these people are? I may not know them, but I have faith that they exist. Similarly, I may not know Krishna, but evidence suggests He, or She, or They may exist; so I may wish to investigate further. Has this Krishna left any clues, writings, or teachings? According to various authorities, there are clues in the Vedas - in the 9 million+ words in the Rig, Sama, Yajur and Atharva Vedas; the Upanishads; the Puranas; the Mahabharata and Bhagavad Gita; and the Ramayana. According to tradition, these texts are taught by guru. Guru comes from a long line of disciplic succession where purity is monitored by people. Guru has been taught by his teachers which sections of the texts mentioned in Veda are relevant to this day and age, and which sections were more relevant in the distant past. Guru must understand the essential spirit of the teachings.

***

As well as opening the temple in Dublin, Head Monk Tribhuvanatha's main service to the mission of his spiritual teacher was to organise Hare Krishna festivals. From 1994 to

1996 he organised seven festivals in Cork, Limerick, and Galway cities. We would go to the location about a week before the event and distribute thousands of leaflets to people on the main streets. We put up posters all around town. We also distributed books and welcomed people to the events – always with a smile.

Usually around 300 to 400 people would attend these festivals, to experience Vedic culture, philosophy, music and food. They were joyous events, and really exchanges of love. Everyone was very happy. The soul's fundamental baseline is taking part in loving service with other souls, and these events gave everyone who took part a real sense of brotherly and sisterly camaraderie. It was evident in their faces - the joy of being alive, free and active. Here at the events, no one was after the money of the festival goers. No one was intensely waiting for material results. For a few hours, the festival became a village and a home.

The standard formula was: (1) kirtan chant music; (2) a philosophical lecture; (3) kirtan chant music where everyone is encouraged to dance, and (4) a vegetarian feast during which attendees chat with the Hare Krishna devotees spontaneously and naturally, if they so desired.

Tribhuvanatha Das was sincere, focused, and knowledgeable when he lectured. (See the Appendix for lecture details). Tribhuvanatha, although brought up until the age of 16 in County Longford in Ireland, spoke with his own unique world accent, a linguistic fusion created from his time spent with Irish, English, American, African, and Indian god-brothers. As a teenager from 1969, he had been touched by spiritual love and then later fashioned by raw austerity, and that all shone through when he gave a teaching.

Tribhuvanatha Das

In 1965, an elderly Indian monk had departed from Kolkata on a cargo ship, with a message of bhakti, the love of the soul. Having begun to share this love with people in North America during the late '60s, six adults and one baby had arrived in London in 1968 with a mission to pass on this love to people in Europe.

Tribhuvanatha, as an Irish boy in London, seized the opportunity and had become infected with some of this Krishna bhakti love. He'd quickly become a leader and organiser of others, while the six original adults - three couples - were called around the world on other missions.

Tribhuvanatha's parents first heard about the whole thing by seeing their son being interviewed on television as the **'Head of the Hare Krishna movement in England'**.

He was 18!

The early devotees of Krishna were soldiers in the war against Maha-Maya (illusion). Their battlefield was the city streets, and they carried war-drumming weapons. A saffron-robed regiment chanting on the streets for 8 or 10 hours a day was not uncommon. Bloodied hands, due to drumming or clashing cymbals, were frequent injuries. So, Tribhuvanatha had lived his young manhood in this fashion, and he oozed warmth, sincerity, and appreciation. If we have been touched by a soul who has been touched by a great soul, this love is the most valuable thing in the entire world – in the entire universe. Nothing else even comes close.

Canto 6, Chapter 3, Verse 32 of the Srimad Bhagavatam states, with Saint Sukadeva Goswami talking to a powerful ruler:

"My dear King, the chanting of the holy name of the Lord is able to uproot even the reactions of the greatest sins.

Therefore the chanting of the sankirtan movement is the most auspicious activity in the entire universe. Please try to understand this so that others will take it seriously."

San-kirtan is the chanting of holy names for the benefit of everyone everywhere. If you would like to find out more about the Vedic and Vaishnava angle on this, then please see the Appendix.

Going Saffron

One month in '94 Tribhuvanatha called me aside and said I was ready to go into saffron. This is the orange-coloured cloth of a monk, which only a monk can wear. There was no event or ceremony… Monk Giri simply gave me some dye and a bucket, and told me what to do. One buys the deep orange dye in a shop specialising in sewing, knitting and fabrics. So my white dhoti robes became saffron, and I was now a real brahmachari student monk… at least in dress. I would have to work on the consciousness and inner world in the years to come. Our Head Monk's modus operandi came from what he was brought up with at the start of the movement in Europe in 1969. Temples nowadays have more formalities and regulations in this regard.

Summer 1994

As a 19-year-old student monk wearing saffron robes, I travelled over land and sea from Dublin to Brussels. In the southern part of Belgium, in the Ardennes forest region, Hare Krishna devotees had purchased a period stone chateau in 1980. Arriving by train at the local village of Barvaux, I asked a passerby:

"Excuse moi, ou est l'office du tourism, s'il vous plait." (My attempt at the French language from what I remembered in school.) After a bemused pause, the woman quickly pointed a finger down one road, and then disappeared from my vicinity with panicked urgency.

My flowing orange robes caught a final gust of wind as I entered the tourism office. I immediately started speaking English - as English-speakers tend to do - and cheerfully asked the one staff member which road I should walk down to get to the Hare Krishna temple. With an incredulous stare of disgust, the woman curtly responded that that she had no comment to make on the religious cult group that were *not* registered with their agency. Shock. I had never come across a tourism official so rude before. Also, I knew that the temple had regular tourist coach tour groups coming on guided tours, so I just assumed the local tourism office was on-board. It turns out the devotees dealt with private tour companies coming from the Netherlands and Flanders, as members of the government in Wallonia (like the French government) tended to be suspicious of groups they saw as being religious cults. Anyway, I wasn't welcome there, so I hastily retreated and began wandering down the street. Fortunately, after a few moments a Krishna devotee also on the way to the temple (which was 7km away) saw me, stopped, and offered a lift.

The castle had a fairy-tale air about it. Complete with towers, turrets, and a winding stone stairway with tall damp steps in one wing, it looked like an image from a children's storybook. The principal entrance way had a grand, sweeping staircase and stone floors. Underfloor heating, surprisingly cosy, had been installed after the devotees bought the property. Old wood wall carvings and elegant framed paintings were everywhere. I stayed for several days for lectures (all in English) and enjoyed the spiritual association of Hare Krishna people from around Europe. One morning at 4.00am I entered the men's communal shower room where 30 men were in a dozy silence, fumbling around with soap and tooth paste. I remember the contrast and transformation when I brought in a Sony tape player with built-in speaker. The grave voice of Srila Prabhupad started playing, cutting through the inertia. Pra'bhu'pad was a monk, swami and spiritual reformer who lectured on the essence of spiritual life.

The next day at the Q&A period of the lecture, I asked one visiting swami a question. I was bowled over by his gentleness when he responded to me in front of 200 people. Hare Krishna swamis would usually address young brahmachari monks in the manner of a stern 1950s school teacher. But this swami was choosing to show another example that we offer humble respect to everyone, and that we should see ourselves as ready to serve everyone.

September 1994

BD was a name that echoed around the ashram corridors of these islands at the Atlantic edge of Northern Europe: a man not to be messed with. He was brought up in a tough neighbourhood of Glasgow. I had heard his deep, resonating, masculine voice giving lectures and chanting on tape cassettes. In '93 and '94, there were leader boards for Hare Krishna book distribution around Europe, and at this time Scotland was number one in all of Europe.

There was a rumour going around that BD's men were all yogis in their past lives, and 'yogi' here does not refer to slim women in trendy attire. Rather, we are talking about a thin, gaunt man with long, matted hair, seated in the Himalayan snow with a meditative, grave and renounced aura about him.

In the International Society for Krishna Consciousness one is encouraged to seek out living spiritual teachers and find a connection with a guru. BD seemed exciting to my 19-year-old self, so I requested to visit the Scottish temple. My stay there lasted for 10 days in September 1994. This was to be the most military-like experience I would ever have.

The temple was situated in a village midway between Glasgow and Edinburgh. Every day we would drive out on the mission to collect donations and distribute books. When I was shown what to do, I was immediately uncomfortable. In Ireland, we were doing the general international standard of holding a small stack of books in one's hand, showing them to people on the street and then selling the book for a donation.

In Scotland, they would hold an official-looking charity board and flash images of poor and underprivileged, hungry children. When someone gave a donation to help the underprivileged, then they'd be given a small book. Although it is true that there is something called Hare Krishna Food for Life, and some Food for Life volunteers do actually feed children in famine and war zones, in this case the whole set-up just seemed like it was stretching the truth. The money was being used both for the Scottish centre and to feed people which, I hear, is what modern charities often do. As far as I understand, it's common for a modern charity to spend a huge amount of its budget on advertising, salaries, office expenses, etc, with only a small portion going to actually help people. So, although the Scottish temple was collecting money to feed people, some of the money was also helping to keep their religious centre open and to print spiritual books. The international standard of presenting the books straightforwardly and telling people that the book was about ancient wisdom, bhakti-yoga and finding inner contentment seemed more to the point to my idealistic self. Some people disagree. They say that as the 'board method' was getting very good results with the quantity of books distributed, and then the results speak for themselves.

There was always a brief pep talk by BD around about 5:10am. If you can imagine a Scottish accent: "So, Little Timmy doesn't like our methods. However, this is what we do, and it works," said BD sternly to the 30+ soldiers in the assembly. I stayed quiet.

Next that morning, everyone was to chant the Hare Krishna mantra on traditional wooden japa beads. This is an individual meditation where one murmurs the mantra to oneself out loud. One may sit, pace up and down slowly, or go for a walk. I prepared to go outdoors.

"Where do you think you're going?" demanded one man. "Outside," I flashed with my eyes, wondering what was going on.

"BD Prabhu says it's Maya (illusion) to go away from the devotees. We all stay here together."

"Huh?!" said my eyes... starting to get uncomfortable with the idea of over 30 people all squeezed into the room on top of each other. The temple room was not too big at all. In Ireland, I was used to wandering around in nature – free as a bird – doing my personal meditation floating past mature trees. So I did my best to follow orders. After four hours of morning sadhana, chanting, lecture, and meditation, the troops were sent out to fight Maya.

There were a few eccentricities. BD said he didn't want anyone speeding, so the temple had a fleet of old Citroën CXs – the car shaped like a little turtle – which didn't have the capacity to go fast at all with their tiny little engines. Monks filed into these little cars ready to drive to various towns or cities around Scotland. One would get one's brunch on a huge stainless steel plate, sit in the car, and then do more Japa (chanting) as we drove. They had a rule that we couldn't eat until 20 minutes before arriving at the destination, whether it be Edinburgh, Aberdeen, Dundee, or wherever. So, there we were, looking at all the food going cold. Then at some point the senior man in the car would give the go ahead for us to start eating our main meal for the day. After eating, we would wash our hands with water spray by opening the windows of the still-driving car. In Vedic culture it's seen as important to wash one's hands and mouth before and after eating. But as we were racing to get out on the front lines, we didn't have time to stop the car, so we had to wash on the go.

We arrived in the town, guns blazing, like Navy SEALs parachuting into enemy territory. There was a sense that the souls here were lost in illusion and that we were coming to liberate them. At times, though, people did question what we were doing.

***

I remember once in some busy streets on a Saturday afternoon, one of the Scottish temple charity collectors had annoyed somebody. This member of the public had petitioned a police officer, and then someone shouted out that the police were after us, and then I found myself running down the road and hiding from the law in a crowd of shoppers.

In the Scottish temple one evening, I was manhandled into what they called an initiation ceremony. I was carried by a few men and dunked into a bath of cold water. I took the thing fairly okay, in a joking spirit, but I didn't tell them that I also thought it was all a little weird.

The temple residents worked long hours out collecting donations and distributing literature. One day we were out all day and I really felt like having a break, but I was told breaks weren't allowed, so I sneaked away and found myself in a larger-sized wheelchair toilet of some McDonalds, where I sat down on the floor in the corner furthest from the just-cleaned toilet and closed my eyes for a nap. I slept there for half an hour.

Years later BD was investigated by the society's international governing body, and it was decided he was performing practices inappropriate for a guru. He later left the society. For my own part, I was delighted to return to Ireland and taste freedom. However, I will always hold some appreciation and gratitude for my 10 days of military education. But I wouldn't like to repeat the experience.

Telling this story of my trip to Scotland, I'm not intending to criticise anyone. BD organised and promoted the distribution of many hundreds of thousands of copies of spiritual literature, which is good news. As is said in Hare Krishna circles, this is the material world. There are good things and bad things all over the place. Duality.

Back in Ireland

Approaching random strangers on public streets, appearing happy and confident, and striking up conversations was challenging for a shy boy like me. To sell books like 'The Science of Self-Realisation' or 'The Perfection of Yoga' took a lot of people-based focus.

We would travel all around the country, and every month we'd meet up for some rejuvenation in the temple. Once, at one of our conference get-togethers, I said to Head Monk Tribhuvanatha that I couldn't go on like this. It was too difficult.

"The people we meet on the streets are busy with their lives. They don't have time or interest to listen to Vedic philosophy."

He responded with gravity and kindness. He told me that it wasn't *that* hard. I don't have to act. He told me that I should just talk frankly and honestly to people – from the heart – and that Krishna would do the rest. He said, "Just be yourself, and everything will be fine." He was so encouraging. Compassion is a huge concept and feeling that one associates with Jesus, Buddha or Krishna, but on that day, I could see a spark of this in his eyes. It wasn't just his words, but his whole presence and intention, like I had found someone who actually cared about others.

***

Sports are not commonly performed by ashram resident young monks, but if they are – in tradition – wrestling and swimming are what *brahmacharis* will do. We somehow decided to have wrestling matches on one of the visits to the main temple for the young monks who were travelling around the country and preaching. As the smallest of all the men, I was correctly matched up with Mick Duff – who was the second smallest. So, we were wrestling away, with everyone else looking on and cheering. It was the only time I have ever wrestled. Mick was laughing and chuckling the whole time. Being the smallest, it was a bit harder for me, so I was trying my best, which only made Mick laugh all the more. Of course, in laughing he let his guard down, and this gave me the upper hand. I managed to hold him down for a bit, but this only caused him to laugh more. Mick Duff – RIP. Mick had been a singer in a band before joining the temple. Sadly he passed away a few years ago.

***

What were people doing before they joined the temple? What were their backgrounds? It varied. One was pursuing a PhD in chemistry at university; another was a shop assistant; someone was on the social welfare; someone was working on building sites; two of the boys had been singers in bands; someone worked with horses; four of the boys had fathers with successful family businesses, and their time in the temple was life training before they inevitably returned to the family business; two of the girls came straight from secondary school, and that's all that I know of. In the 1980s, there were two brothers who had been in the IRA as active militants carrying out acts of violence, however after donning the robes they renounced their previous ways. One of the two brothers even got married to a woman from a well-off Protestant family. I doubt if the man's previous commanders were too impressed. The BBC made a TV documentary about them ten years into their marriage. Anyhow, people who joined the temple ashrams were from varying backgrounds. What united them was the decision to leave behind their former lives and embark on a spiritual journey.

After we joined the temple, we almost never talked about our previous life. There was a slight undercurrent of a feeling that it was a 'material' topic, and not as important as our new spiritual mission. Years and decades later, I feel that we were also idealistic young people with limited life experience.

- Inish Rath Island -

- A monk in silent meditation -

3

1995:

The Lake Isle of Inish Rath

Early in 1995 I continued to travel all around the island of Ireland distributing books about Krishna consciousness. We sometimes stayed in the backs of vans, other times in the houses of people, or sometimes in the Dublin or Belfast temples. The Belfast temple at this time had a woman called Padma, from Dundalk, as the temple president. In the hundreds of Krishna temples around the world, it was very rare to have a woman temple president. Of the 250 temples at that time, there were only two women presidents. The term 'temple president' comes from the USA. The philosophy and culture of the movement comes from ancient India, but the society first began international expansion from North America, and so the term was first adopted there. The Belfast temple was quite vibrant at that time, and Padma (Patricia Rafferty) performed a wonderful service, along with the other women there. There was one older male monk. This temple was always strikingly clean and tidy. I did not stay for long in this temple, just for one night at a time, on occasion, over a period of 18 months. So I can't go into too much detail about it, other than to say there was always a nice atmosphere about the place when I stayed there.

***

Book distribution, as a service, is marvellous and revealing. First, in order to do the activity at all one is forced to read the literature one is distributing with urgency, almost in desperation. An honest man simply can't go in front of someone and tell them he has wonderful books and suggest this person buy one, unless he believes this himself. One must read the books with a prayerful passion, trying to enter deeply into the meaning. The books we distributed were either direct translations of sacred texts, or commentaries on these ancient wisdom books. If we were in Galway (or wherever) we would walk up to the person and say something like "Hey, are you from Galway, or elsewhere?" If and when the person responds, then one gives another question, and all the time one is trying figure out the person, and guess things about them. Is he or she a student, business person, office employee, farmer, brick-layer, solicitor or carpenter? Then one attempts to say something to relate the book to the person. Does this person ever get stressed? This book can help with stress. Does this person get too busy at times, and need time to reflect? A basic human need is to love, and be loved, so the book distributor's mind is calculating rapidly and trying to pick the words of choice to relate the book to this particular individual. Furthermore, one is trying to be prayerful internally, remembering that one is doing a voluntary service to share good with the world. But, at the same time, we needed to get money to print the book, and the van we were driving around in had expenses, so income was important. The whole thing, however, is done in a mood of love, so one really wants the person to read the book and be benefitted. If someone really had no money, we would just give it to them for free, but we would really have to ensure they had a sincere interest. There is no point in someone taking one, and throwing it in the bin 10 minutes later.

***

One afternoon, while attending a Sunday Love Feast in the Dublin temple, someone pointed out Glen Hansard to me. Glen was a singer and I remembered him from the 1990 film

'The Commitments'. I was helping serve out the meal, so everyone was sitting on the floor. I remember looking down as I was serving, and I had a quick exchange with Glen. He was clearly in bliss to be there at that moment. It turns out Ravinol Chambers (one of the new brahmachari monks) used to be old pals with Glen. Some years later Glen and his friend Markéta won an Oscar for Best Original song at the Academy Awards, for the music on their 2007 film, 'Once'. They were the stars of that year – so honest, real and down-to-earth; they connected with their art as an experience to better themselves and contribute something meaningful to humanity. Glen included a quick shot of the chanting of Hare Krishna at the beginning of the film 'Once'.

***

Some months later, Tribhuvanatha Das had something new for me. He asked if I could go to help out at Inish Rath Island, also known as Krishna Island. The Pandava Sena was a fairly new youth group of British Indians, and the youth – aged about 16 to 24 – were going to Krishna Island for a retreat. So, I went for a few days, not knowing that I was to live there for years to come.

Inish Rath Island

Inish Rath Island is a 22-acre (9-hectare) wooded lake island, situated in the River Erne system. Lough Erne has 154 islands between the upper and lower lakes, a few of which are inhabited. (For readers who are not Irish, 'Lough' is pronounced in the same way as 'Loch' in Scotland, and I don't know how the spelling 'ough' came to be). In November 1854 the 3rd Earl of Crom Castle, John Crichton, sold the island to the Honourable Henry Cavendish Butler of Dublin for the sum of £643. From 1856 Henry had an imposing residence built in a central and raised location on the island, and within a few years of the construction of the house the Ordinance survey map shows a network of paths, a walled garden and a pier on the island. This layout from the late 1850s remains to this day. Henry held the position of the sheriff of County Cavan, and later the sheriff of County Fermanagh.

This same Butler-Cavendish family owned the island until 1953, and by this time the house had fallen into a state of disrepair. The next owners were Lieutenant Konstanty Scheunert and his wife Ruth. Konstanty was a Polish exile after WWII and had become one of Northern Ireland's richest men in the 1950s through his business pursuits. In a 1959 interview with the Belfast Telegraph he said: "I came to live here on Lough Erne because it reminds me of the lake country of Poland where I can never return… I like the people here. I like their easy-going way of life. And I think it's the most beautiful spot in the world." The Scheunerts had found the property in an advanced stage of neglect and they set about restoring and modernising it, including the introduction of electricity and oil-fired central heating. Following Konstanty's death in 1970 the island was offered for sale again, and was soon purchased by the Mortons, who after a few summers and winters of island-living sold Inish Rath to Lockwood Construction Ltd. in 1975. When a plan to develop the property for tourism didn't come to fruition, this company sold the island to Sam and Jo Crawford in 1978.

***

In 1984 a group of Hare Krishna devotees were looking for a rural community in which to settle and live. One day, as they were driving past an auctioneer's office, a salesman was posting a notice and images of an intriguing-looking place in his shop window. So they went in immediately and were informed that a lake island with a large old house was on the market. They quickly purchased the island for £125,000. Prithu Das – who had been born in the Netherlands and brought up in Germany – was the man in charge and he made the decision to buy the island. The previous owners were concerned about the ongoing Troubles in Northern Ireland (particularly after a well-known supermarket owner was kidnapped by the IRA), and they wanted to return to their native England.

In order to raise funds, the young residents of the temple sold landscape paintings and nature artwork. It was a type of idealistic spiritual communism, working for the group, rather than for themselves. The island was purchased by ordinary people, pooling their money and resources. A few years later, these young men and women began marrying and setting up their own households, so they needed to hold onto their own private money. However just at that time in the mid-eighties they all contributed communally. The island is now owned by a charity.

***

In 1985 the devotees began the process of transforming the property into a temple, culminating in a lavish Open Day in July 1986. The first Open Day was attended by several thousand local people who enjoyed helicopter rides, pageantry, drama, music, and a Vedic fire sacrifice. This fire 'yajna' is a ceremony going back millennia where names of God are chanted to bring auspiciousness to all. Wood is burned, with the priest occasionally pouring clarified butter into the flames. The burning area is surrounded by coconuts, bananas, pineapples, vegetables and flowers. One gives thanks for all these items, and one can meditate that the fire is burning away sin, karma and bad intentions. In our county of 60,000 people, I often still meet people who attended this family day out: That magical day when a rural area of the island of Ireland was transformed into the exotic East.

***

The razzmatazz continued with another Open Day in 1987. The original intention was to make this into an annual event.

Unfortunately, though, there was an undercurrent of dissatisfaction among many ashram residents, and two camps opposed to each other formed. There were allegations of unnecessary, lavish spending of the temple's money, which led to disagreements and arguments, and this led to the breakdown of relationships.. Devotees revolted and petitioned the Governing Body of the Society to request the leadership to leave the project. So, the island – after a few years – became emptied of people. The temple deities and altar worship ceremonies remained, but by the time I first visited in 1993, the place had the air of an introverted private ashram with a skeleton crew. I suppose people will always go through successions of learning experiences as well as challenges in communication which often result in change.

For the past 30 years the temple comes alive for festivals, events and most Sundays, and then quietens down in between. I lived there during some quiet periods, and I enjoyed the tranquillity of living on a remote island at the edge of Western Europe.

***

For most of the 1990s, access to the island was only by rowing boat. A heavy brass bell, 35cm (14 inches) tall, hung from a tree branch at the pier. The pilgrim or resident desiring to journey across the lake waters to reach the island would ring the bell and any able-bodied man available could answer the call and row the boat across.

Inish Rath is situated along a former pilgrimage route. When the country had wolves roaming through dense forest 1400 years ago, pilgrims rowed past this island on their way to Station Island on Lough Derg, forty miles to the north. Even to this day, Lough Derg still serves as a place of spiritual retreat. I have met many people over the years who've endured a weekend of fasting, sleep deprivation, and murmuring on rosary beads at Lough Derg. In the Vedic tradition, the yogi or sadhu is advised to sleep less to help give more time to sadhana, spiritual practice. At the same time, forced sleep deprivation beyond the realisation of the practitioner is regarded as being unhealthy. But reducing eating and sleeping to a minimum is highly regarded.

***

Our typical day on the island began by arising between 3.00 and 4.00am, showering, applying tilak (sacred clay markings on the forehead) and dressing in orange robes. Next, we sang kirtan music and offered prayers from 4.30am to 5.15am. This was followed by chanting the Hare Krishna mantra on wooden beads in a quiet meditative manner. Inish Rath follows the same standard morning programme I had experienced at Bhaktivedanta Manor. There was, however, a difference in numbers of attendees. On the island we'd have three, five or nine enthusiasts for the morning programme, with five or six people being a typical turnout. In the Manor there would be 28, 35 or 47 people present every morning, with extra attendees for special events.

From 7.00am there is the *Greeting of the Deities*. In 1970, George Harrison had helped to arrange a grand and enlivening piece of music with Hare Krishna devotees in London, and a recording of this song is played in all ISKCON temples around the world at 7.00am.

Afterwards there is the singing of a song respecting the spiritual teachers. This is followed by an in-depth study of one verse of the 18,000 verse Srimad Bhagavatam, a primary Vedic text. I feel blessed to have had the opportunity to spend a few thousand mornings like this between the 1990s and into the first years of new millennium. I am deeply grateful for Tribhuvanatha's gentle leadership. My life seemed to seamlessly flow from city preacher to rural island monk. There was no major plan, but rather just the freedom to allow people to be where they should be.

***

My time on the island was a happy time. There were moments when I could hardly believe my good fortune. After the austerities of being on the urban front lines, the challenges of island life were mild in comparison. The ancient worship of large, three-dimensional archa-vigraha forms of Radha Krishna, the feminine and masculine Divine, involves the offering of succulent, delicious foodstuffs to the Deities on a daily basis. Traditionally in a temple the many visiting pilgrims accept a tiny portion of this food after it has been sanctified. But I found myself on a remote island on the edge of Europe with this sumptuous Krishna maha-prasad food available for pilgrims daily – but no one around to eat it.

Accordingly, I ate like a ***king*** between the ages of 20 and 26. I was continuously swimming in culinary heaven. How I did not get fat at all back then is a physiological mystery. I guess my young age, arising early, and the fact that I was living and working in the same place, always on call, and never idle – all combined to keep me physically thin in spite of eating voraciously.

Abstinence

A student monk abstains from (1) eating meat, fish or eggs; (2) sexual connections; (3) intoxication; and (4) gambling.

As previously mentioned, I was already eating like a king, so not eating meat wasn't an issue, plus I was familiar with the concept of ahimsa (non-violence). Also, many Hare Krishna people are very good cooks. I didn't have any money to gamble anyway; and I personally had never smoked, consumed alcohol, or taken drugs, nor have I yet had any interests here. Dealing with one's relationships and the inbuilt desire to find a mate is generally a greater challenge for most people. I remember once seeing an attractive photograph in an English magazine which promoted sustainable living and eco-friendliness. Someone had left the magazine behind in the temple. It showed a good-looking young couple sitting and enjoying life in a summer flower meadow. I looked at that photo, and thought "Oh, I'd like to be in a situation like that in the future."

I gazed at that image several times, as weeks and months went by. But while one is a young monk one must try to put this aside, and try to put time into discovering oneself first. One tries to do this by keeping the mind and body busy all the time.

Hare Krishna Clothing

When I lived on the island I wore the saffron robes of a monk practically every day. Married men wear white or other colours. Do Hare Krishna people *have to* wear Indian clothes? No. But they can choose to do so, especially in the temple. A temple resident would be expected to wear this traditional Indian clothing. According to the tradition and beliefs, a dhoti and a sari are clothing present in the eternal spiritual world. This is the viewpoint of shastra, or the ancient Vedic texts. Once a devotee leaves temple life, they choose for themselves whether to follow these customs, but it is common for Hare Krishna followers who live outside to wear the Indian clothes in the temple or if attending a large event. When Srila Prabhupad came to the USA initially the new followers just wore their normal Western clothing. On a visit to India in 1967, the swami brought back some saris for the young women, but men carried on wearing their usual clothes. Later on the new devotees of Krishna themselves preferred to experiment and wear traditional robes. A 'dhoti' is a lower garment for men. A 'kurta' is a shirt top. Women have a sari dress, which is an enormous length of multi-coloured cotton with exotic designs, wrapped in a particular fashion. A choli is a dainty upper garment which is largely covered by a section of the sari.

The different clothing can act as a kind of priestly uniform which can help the practitioner and others to identify him or her as connected with Vedic cultural traditions. A sari has a head covering which can act to help allow the woman or girl to appear more modest. Head coverings also have a practical application – it holds the hair when cooking, and it can provide protection from the sun or from insects, for example.

The girls can wear the traditional clothes in different ways depending on their personality, motivations, or the local culture. For example, a young woman might like to reveal more of her body, especially around the waist area, and display beautiful jewellery. Another woman or girl might be dressing more modestly, showing less or none of her waist, arms or shoulders, or having less jewellery.

When Hare Krishna expanded in the West in the 1970s the women tended to look more religious, using the head coverings and dressing more modestly. As time went on, and many members integrated more into Western culture, women and men tended to mix local European-based customs into their dress codes. In some traditions (like ISKCON / Hare Krishna) a woman wearing a bindi (a red dot in the centre of her forehead) means that she is a married woman. This is a useful indicator to young men that they should not be giving her romantic attention.

***

In August 1995, Śivarāma Swami and BD, the Army General from Scotland, came to visit for a few days. Śivarāma Swami was the GBC (Governing Body Commissioner) for Great Britain and Ireland. In the Roman Catholic Church, this would be like the equivalent of the Cardinal for this region. A tall man with flowing orange robes, he spoke with a deep, commanding voice. His Canadian grizzly bear exterior masked a gentle panda underneath. However, he would seldom show this tender face publicly. Born in Hungary in 1949, he emigrated to Montreal with his family at the age of seven. And in 1989 he returned to Hungary as a guru to teach Vedic philosophy and Krishna consciousness there.

BD was an enormous man with a deep military voice. There is a tradition in Vedic culture that when one eats from a plate, a portion of your consciousness is subtly transferred into that food –that is, whatever food remains on the plate. If a holy person happens to leave some remnants on his or her plate, and one gets to eat these leftovers, one is considered to have imbibed or absorbed some devotional and spiritual consciousness. One is blessed.

When serving the meals, I inadvertently transferred some food that had been on BD's plate onto the Swami's plate. Later on, I was summoned up to the room of the Scottish devotee. Having been made aware of what had happened, he looked at me with intense burning fury. How dare I offend Swami like this, he demanded. He considered himself junior to Swami, so Swami shouldn't eat his leftovers. He threatened to personally kill me if I ever made such an offence again. He didn't sound like he was joking. His booming voice displayed shocking gravity. Guru means heavy. A guru is not meant to mollycoddle a student with flowers, incense, and sweet words. The closest example that you might be aware of is how an army sergeant might train a new military recruit, with discipline that would be considered over-the-top elsewhere. Traditionally, a guru will often speak strongly to get a message across. Sivarama Swami was unaware of these goings on, and I don't consider BD really intended to murder me, but he certainly wasn't flowery-light and cheery when speaking to me. I'm actually thankful to him for this kind of interaction. It *'makes a man of you'*, some might say.

Temple life was regulated. At 8.30 every morning, I brought out the breakfast (at times when there was a crowd, I cooked extra). Then I rang a big brass bell, and all the residents assembled, took their seats on the floor with stainless steel plates and I moved around, stooped over, and served everyone. Generally, there were around a dozen people. But sometimes there could be up to 30 or 40 people present for special occasions.

At 1.00pm we would all assemble again and feasted like a happy family. For the early morning programme and two mealtimes, punctuality was impressive by general Irish or Indian standards. Residents could help themselves to some Krishna-prasad (sanctified food), in the evening, if they wished. However, breakfast and lunch were strictly communal affairs where people gathered together in a relaxed, informal setting to chat and enjoy succulent food.

Outside of mealtimes, the residents were engaged in various temple services. On Inish Rath Island there has only really been one department continuously existing since the day the temple was founded – the Deity Department – which manages the daily altar seva (service). Someone was on duty from 3.30am daily and there were seven ancient arati ceremonies offered to Radha Krishna throughout the day from the early morning until 8.30pm.

From the time the temple was founded in 1986, most residents have been involved in maintaining the puja, or altar ceremonies and offerings. These ceremonies are formal and age-old opportunities to help people slow down, pause, and be grateful. One meditates on Radha Krishna as the feminine / masculine divine source. Radha is also called Hara, which becomes Ha'ray in the vocative tense of Sanskrit grammar. This word is generally spelled 'Hare', although that spelling has a non-standard way of expressing the syllable 'ray' in the English language.

Other people maintaining various services tended to come and go, whether they were doing general building maintenance, cleaning, welcoming visitors, operating a boat, chopping wood, and so forth. People stayed at the island temple for a few weeks, months or even a couple of years. This particular temple had ongoing challenges with management and income generation for most of its history as a temple. The temple never had sufficient income to employ anyone full time, so many residents either have had hardly any money, or they have had to go elsewhere to earn an income.

***

Shyamananda Das – formerly Seamus Young – was a local man from a village in County Cavan 20 kilometres away. He served as the Temple President from July 1995 until early 1999. Shyamananda worked very hard to keep the temple going and maintain spiritual standards. An Irish priest-like man who had converted to Eastern ways, he was philosophically inclined, and liked to interact and converse with temple visitors. He was only 23 years old when he took charge of the temple. After secondary school, he had attended third-level college for three years. In his third year he had begun visiting the temple, and the day after he finished the course, he immediately moved into the temple. He was the youngest in his family, and had been largely raised by his older sisters and brothers, as his father had died when little Seamus was age two, and his mother suffered from alcoholism and depression.

He was quite frugal by nature. Cavan people have that reputation of being careful with money. One cold winter we were all feeling the effects of subzero temperatures. He said to me that he could have a plumber rig up a system to heat up a few old cast-iron radiators, or we could have some hot water coming from some tap – but not both. It was one or the other. I suggested we go with some room heat so we we're not freezing all the time and we could heat water on the gas stove in the kitchen. But in the end he opted for his own personal preference – the luxury of warm tap water.

Another time, the light bulb suddenly popped out in the men's shower room one morning. Shyamananda was the first person to enter the non-illuminated little room, and screamed with disgust. A large slug had ventured up the external wall and somehow slithered and squeezed under the window, and Shyamananda had the experience of standing on the slimy mollusc in his bare feet. During the morning chants he sometimes led the singing. He had an intensely unmelodic voice, and yet somehow, with spiritual focus and raw honesty he could make the music sound lyrical and harmonious.

Nature

One day I was sitting on a crop of rocks down by the lake, quietly murmuring mantras. A slender dog-sized mammal emerged from the water and came walking towards me. Having been brought up in the suburbs of Dublin, I was completely unfamiliar with the native wildlife of the Irish countryside. "Is this beast going to run, jump and grab my neck?" was my first thought. The eyes of the very wild animal connected with mine, and we looked at each other. Our worlds stood still. Then, after due consideration, perhaps he thought I was too big to attack, so he moved his head, shrugged, turned around, and returned from whence he came. Sometime later I discovered this creature was an otter. Maybe due to a past-life I have a deeply embedded memory of being a herbivore chomping away at some juicy and lush grass, only to be chased and attacked by a predator, who went for my neck. This might explain why I don't really warm up to the predator-types that bark, howl and eat meat. Maybe. When I watch African safari documentaries, I'm rooting for the springboks and baby buffalo.

***

In a temple we often don't have many possessions, which can include not having a torch when one actually could do with one. One evening in October I had to cross over to the mainland for some purpose or other. The journey down to the boat quay was dark and quiet. Unseen clouds covered the sky, shielding any light available from the moon and stars. I was forced to proceed slowly, trying to make out trees in the gloom. I wasn't too keen on getting a tree branch in my face, or worse, in my eyes. And then it struck. A loud sound came out of nowhere; a roar, only a few metres from me, just off the woodland path. My first thought was that it was a leopard. I had a feeling maybe they could swim, like jaguars. So, in half a second, with heart pounding furiously, I reasoned that a leopard had escaped from some zoo, and made its way through the countryside in search of prey. As it proceeded, it killed and devoured sheep at night, and then swam over to the island. So here he was now, just behind the bushes and trees, merely a few feet away from me. My body went into overdrive with adrenaline pumping everywhere, heart racing and beating like a heavy metal percussion instrument, as I braced myself for the attack. My slow walk turned into a speed walk, and then a run, as the beast roared again. A break in the trees allowed welcome patches of dim light, giving more visibility, which allowed me to up-gear to a sprint. At the lake I jumped into the rowing boat and cast off - desperately trying to get some distance from a position that would enable a death pounce from a big cat. In a minute I was clear. I didn't let down my guard but proceeded with haste and caution. I had escaped the leopard. Again, being a city boy, I was totally ignorant of the breeding season and mating habits of deer. In October, it is customary for a buck to make mating noises meant to attract a doe. What I had thought was a big cat, was actually a male fallow deer, bellowing out an impressive masculine roar, as he tried in earnest to attract a female partner. Whoops. City boy.

***

For most of the time when I lived in the temple, I had no direct day-to-day manager to supervise and check over everything I did during the day. Of course, I wanted to pull my weight, and contribute, so I was practically always active cleaning, answering the phone, helping in the kitchen, assisting day-visitors with their visit, etc. Occasionally, I would do something spontaneous. One hot summer day I swam over to the island due south of us, a six-acre island covered in woodland. I wandered around there, imagining living in a little eco-house there in the future. It was an idyllic setting: sun, water, sky, air, trees, freedom.

Another day, again one October during the deer mating season, I crossed over to the mainland. Again, as before, I had no torch, and the sky was pitch-black. On the mainland, across a large field, I could hear what sounded like galloping, and then the violent clash of antlers. Two bucks were fighting for mating rights, and sounds of the struggle were reverberating around the night sky, and could even be felt through solid ground. My imagination got the better of me, and I had a sudden vision of being impaled by the wild animals due to accidentally getting caught between the two gladiators. Relying only on sound, and with senses tuned in like a primordial hunter-gatherer, I waited until I heard the antler-clash in the far corner of the field over to one side. And then I ran for my life up through the middle of the battlefield, jumping over a fence to safety.

***

Peacocks have a lifespan of between 15 to 25 years and several males and peahens were introduced to the island in the mid-eighties. They've been reproducing, and some of the peachicks make it into adulthood, although many get taken by otters or minks. As a defensive measure, they sleep high up in trees at night. Peacocks, as is well known, are extremely handsome. I've often seen them look at reflections of themselves. Mother

Nature can have a cruel side also. One day a migrating black-backed gull appeared to have damaged one of his wings, and he had landed, attempting to recuperate. As this was a 'foreigner' on the island, peacocks ganged up on him, and were pecking away at his body. It was disconcerting to see a symbol of elegance and charm in Nature acting like a common bully, but peacocks are known to be territorial, and don't take kindly to strangers. Even the most majestic symbols of beauty have their instincts, and in this case, it wasn't one of their finer moments.

- Children in India -

- An ox at Krishna Valley, Hungary -

4

1996:

India, Hungary and

Island Days

Just before Christmas '95, I spent some time away from the island to sell books and collect money for an India pilgrimage trip. I had always been a net contributor to the mission, but this time a percentage of the takings paid for the airplane ticket and inexpensive ashram accommodation in the holy places. India has many interesting holy shrines and temples for the pilgrim or traveller to visit. To see Krishna, go to Vrindavan; for Rama, go to Ayodhya; for yogis, there is Rishikesh at the foothills of the Himalayas, a city where meat and alcohol are banned; for Buddhists, Bodh Gaya; for Sikhs, the Golden Temple in Punjab; for Shiva – Varanasi, one of the oldest continually inhabited cities in the world; for followers of Jagannatha (Krishna in a certain esoteric form), go to Jagannatha Puri; for kirtan (mantra music) go to Shri Krishna Chaitanya at Mayapur; for the largest gathering of human beings on the planet, go to the Kumbha Mela every 12 years where tens of millions of pilgrims camp out in tents and attend religious functions, etc.

Do all Hare Krishna devotees around the world go to India? Many do, but it is a personal choice. Some might never go;

some have only gone once or twice; and some make it an annual pilgrimage.

***

India

On the way to India, I had to change flights in Dubai. I remember looking out the windows of this airport and seeing rolling sand dunes and white-robed sheikhs standing by their shiny new limousines. The Dubai airport at that time appeared more provincial and Middle Eastern as compared with the major international and cosmopolitan hub that it has become today.

Arriving in India and walking out on the street in Delhi for the first time was a cultural hurricane and an assault on the senses. I was wearing the orange robes of a brahmachari student monk. Instantly, people came towards me to talk: sellers, children, and taxi drivers. I started to give away apples to kids while listening to adults babbling in Hindi that I didn't understand, simultaneously noticing monkeys swinging from lampposts, long-horned cows trundling by, rickshaws, car horns, bells, shouting, heat, smells, and exotic food aromas. Noticing I looked visibly overwhelmed, one of my travelling companions, Sharma Das, offered words of advice, which could be summarised as 'politely but firmly ignore everyone'. The four of us made our way to a train station. Sharma had been a lead singer in a small professional band in England before coming over to Ireland.

Peter was brought up in Lisburn. His father was an *Orangeman* – that is, a type of person in Northern Ireland who identifies as being *extremely* British. The Orange Order was formed in 1795 and its members are enthusiastic and fervent supporters of the British Crown. And then there was Rachel, from Dublin. She had a very nice singing voice. Following Sharma, we boarded a train to Kolkata. Later, I wondered if Sharma had bribed a train staff member, or maybe we had just paid more for a different ticket. We were led to some bunk beds in a compartment, and the train conductor harshly instructed the men on those bunks to leave. So, we clambered into the bunks, but I was too exhausted and confused to ask what was going on.

The next day I went to use the toilet on the train, and I journeyed down through the carriages through the rattling ever-moving carriage-to-carriage junction areas. I opened a door to discover, to my astonishment, hundreds of people squeezed together cheek-to-cheek, all lying around in a seatless carriage. It seemed to be the class just ahead of the-hanging-onto-the-roof-for-dear-life class. I could see a restroom sign at the far end of the carriage, but to get there I could hardly move any faster than a 90-year-old ballerina, ever so slowly placing my feet and squeezing, contorting and twisting around people, very much trying not to tread on someone. Later, the train stopped in the blistering heat of midday for hours in the middle of nowhere and passengers just waited patiently, stretching or chatting, or simply standing around off the train.

In Kolkata we joined up with thousands of Hare Krishna devotees from around the world for a chanting parade through the city. It was the centenary year celebrating the birth of Srila Prabhupad, the society's founder, in 1896. From there we travelled to Mayapur, 120 kilometres to the south.

Mayapur is in the Bengali countryside, and located here are the world headquarters of the International Society for Krishna Consciousness. The temple complex supports mandirs, shrines, restaurants, shops, workshops for artisans, ashrams for monks, guest houses, offices, gardens, a goshalla for cows and bulls, and there is even a temple elephant wandering around.

***

Mayapur is the holy place dedicated to the divine incarnation, Shri Chaitanya Mahaprabhu. In Bengali Vaishnava theology of recent centuries, Chaitanya is viewed as an esoteric avatar of when Krishna wants to experience the depths of Radha's (Hara's) love. Chaitanya also promoted the Hare Krishna mantra, written below. Found in the Atharva Veda, this is a particularly potent mantra for the present-day. Indeed, the Kali-Saṇṭāraṇa Upaniṣad presents a conversation between demigod Brahma and sage Narada which took place at the beginning of the present age of Kali, 5000 years ago. Narada asks Brahma how souls struggling with limited interest in spiritual life can become purified in these times. "Souls can be purified in this age of Kali by simply chanting names of God," replies Brahma. Narada then asks, "Which names?" and Brahma responds:

"Hare Krishna, Hare Krishna, Krishna Krishna, Hare Hare; Hare Rama, Hare Rama, Rama Rama, Hare Hare. These 16 names, composed of 32 syllables, are the recommended way to counteract the destructive influences of kali-yuga. After having studied the Vedas, we cannot find a method of religion more appropriate for this age than the chanting of the Hare Krishna mantra. Thus, this maha-mantra consisting of 16 names destroys the gross and subtle material coverings of the individual soul. Then the Supreme Lord Krishna will appear in front of this individual soul as the brilliant beams of the sun after the clouds are dispersed."

***

After two weeks of lectures, kirtan (chanting the Hare Krishna mantra with singing and musical instruments) and sadhana (meditation), we travelled back to the north-central part of the subcontinent to Vrindavan, the land of Krishna. I took part in a parikrama where pilgrims walk between 15 and 25 kilometres a day from holy place to holy place singing or meditating using wooden chanting beads as they walk.

Guest speakers would tell stories and histories of bhakti yogis, sages, and/or saintly kings, relating what happened at this place centuries or millennia ago. Over a thousand people took part, sleeping overnight in large tents along the route. Sections for men and women were cordoned off from each other, and every morning hundreds of men would take shower from buckets of cold water. In the showering area men wear a gumsha, or light cotton cloth, around their waist area. I remember the 100 million mosquitoes that came to feast on our legs in the early morning darkness. In tradition, one is recommended to do penance and perform this spiritual pilgrimage barefoot. *"No way am I doing this barefoot,"* I thought, what with snakes, thorns, and rough ground. But on the first day, after we had left behind comfort and civilisation, my cheap flip flops caught in an upturned root of a tree, and they tore apart. It seems I was meant to go barefoot

One day, along the walking route, we passed close to a village of clay huts with roofs of straw far out in the countryside. The natural quaintness was mesmerising. In this place, there was nothing of the modern world – no cars, no machines, no tarmac roads, not even a bicycle. Villagers were all outside, either growing food, tending to cows or making crafts together, and children played and laughed.

The long train of parikrama pilgrims skirted along the outskirts of the village and carried on moving. But I had an urge to spend some moments here. I have never before or since seen such a timeless place, which could have been from any point in history. Was this 3000 BC or 30AD or 1996? Women have been wearing saris and men dhotis during all of this history. Gandhi had spoken lovingly of Indian village life, and here it was in all its quaint glory.

In Vaishnava tradition, the pastoral village of Vrindavan is Krishna's original home. And I now found myself in a magical rustic settlement close to Vrindavan. My reverie was broken with a sudden feeling of emptiness. The sombrero hat which was protecting my white skin and red head was suddenly gone, leaving my head bare to the elements. Young boys had snatched it playfully, and they were now racing around, jumping and joking, laughing and leaping.

There were a few awkward moments where I was wondering what to do… I did need the hat, as without it, my head would be raw-red and roasted in ten minutes. Seeing my challenge, a village elder called the boys over to him, and then he had them humbly return it to me. Breaking from the local dialect, this pleasant old man suddenly turned to me and quoted the first two lines of a Sanskrit verse.

Hey Krishna Karuna Sindhu

Dina Bandhu Jagat Patey

There I stood, with orange robes, pale white, red, and freckled skin – and now reinstated sombrero hat – and I instantly responded with the third and fourth lines of this particular shloka, or verse. Coincidently, I had learned this verse a few weeks previously.

Gopesha Gopika Kanta

Radha Kanta Namo Stutey

The old man's eyes lit up with joy. He was looking at a neophyte pilgrim who had travelled from the cloud forests at the far edge of Northern Eurasia, speaking in the spiritual language of his homeland. For myself, in that place, with those people at that moment, I felt at one with mankind in the land of Krishna. After five minutes I slowly and reluctantly left this magical place, looking over my shoulders several times until the village was out of sight, and I caught up with the long train of pilgrims.

***

After the parikrama (walking pilgrimage) we all headed to the main ISKCON temple in that region for lectures, seminars and kirtan music. One day, I was wandering around in the town's outdoor markets, which sell all manner of Krishna-related products. Suddenly, something brushed roughly and jarringly against my head... and my glasses were gone. I reeled around confused. A monkey had escaped up the market stall canopy tops with the spectacles.

Some local men took pity on my utter bewilderment and offered the monkey a trade for the glasses. A banana was the price demanded by the beast. And then the men kindly retrieved my glasses. However, my flustered, disorientated self grabbed the spectacles, turned around and marched off. In my confusion, I mistook the men for being monkey trainers and miscalculated that they were now going to demand payment from me. Later, on calm reflection, I realised they were simply random passers-by coming to the aid of a religious tourist. Their whole attitude was only giving and not taking. I thank the men for their goodwill and generosity towards me. As you can imagine, I'm embarrassed at my poor attitude.

Return to Lake Isle

Arriving back in the familiar home countries, represented by the bustling Heathrow Airport, I experienced a deeper culture shock than when I had first arrived in India. The intensity of consumerism and secular capitalism was all around me, and now this seemed alien.

I looked into the faces of some passing businessmen and then remembered the smiling residents of the quaint mud-hut village. The two places were worlds apart on so many levels. Returning to misty, cloudy, green Ireland, my mother drove me from Dublin to the Lake Isle of Inish Rath. More culture shock and surprises awaited me. "Where are all the people?" I thought, as my eyes roamed the countryside. Through the car glass windows I looked and felt like I lived at a lonely frontier on the continental edge; as compared with the ancient temples and bustling cities of Bharata (India) which have been embracing throngs of people and animals since time immemorial.

My dear mother stayed the night in the temple and then attended the early part of the morning programme. I was leading the chant using a harmonium. There is something timeless about the Hare Krishna mantra chanted at dawn in the temple. People come and go in our lives. Situations change. Our own body changes in time, but the mantra remains the same. Steady. Dependable. Eternal.

My mother left the room during the service. Later, ashram resident Rachel told me that mother had gone teary-eyed to the ladies' quarters. She told Rachel that she became emotional at the beautiful chanting. Back in Dublin, she may not be able to tell her friends her son is a doctor or a lawyer but now, with a *little* positive pride, she can say, "My son is a monk."

Monkhood… hmmm, the denial of our interest in emotional and physical intimacy with one partner, sacrificing this to open up our love for causes greater than ourselves – the spiritual quest. Or, at least an attempt at this. In Vedic culture it is recommended that the majority of people get married and have families and jobs from a certain age, but from a teenager to mid-twenties, one is in the role of a student. The focus at this time is study, education and preparation. And especially in a spiritual ashram situation, one really leaves aside associating with the opposite sex.

Ideally one should be respectful to – but distant from – the opposite sex. Tribhuvanatha Das had taught us to address all the women as being mother. So even though Rachel was only one year older than me, I would address her as 'Mother Rachel'. In India, and many other parts of the world with ISKCON temples, the Sanskrit term Mataji is used, which is a term of respect for any woman that glorifies her motherly qualities. As one is naturally appreciative of and respectful to one's own birth mother, one is ideally supposed to see other women through the same eyes of respect. Of course, later on in life, one has a different relationship with his wife, but a student monk or 'brahmachari' is meant to be learning kindness as opposed to seeing women as being objects meant for some type of exploitation; whether it be physical or egotistical.

However, many boys in an ashram have a wild medley of conflicting desires. Although the intelligence tells them to put it aside and focus on meditation, the mind remembers a raving fiesta of desire. I had gone to an all-boys' school and I had very little previous contact with girls, but my mind could well remember romantic and sensual scenes from films and television that I saw from ages 15 to 17. According to Vedic philosophy and theology, the conditioned soul in the material world has a desire to enjoy and exploit matter for his or her own selfish benefit, as opposed to becoming the humble servant of God, nature and humanity.

***

Although Veda approves of ananda, or pure spiritual bliss, it suggests that kama (happiness through the senses) needs to be carefully channelled, regulated and controlled. Veda recommends self-realisation.

Bhagavad Gita Chapter 5, Text 24

One whose happiness is within, who is active and rejoices within, and whose aim is inward is actually the perfect mystic. He is liberated in the Supreme, and ultimately he attains the Supreme.

Purport, written by Srila Prabhupad

Unless one is able to relish happiness from within, how can one retire from the external engagements meant for deriving superficial happiness? A liberated person enjoys happiness by factual experience. He can, therefore, sit silently at any place and enjoy the activities of life from within. Such a liberated person no longer desires external material happiness. This state is called brahma-bhūta, attaining which one is assured of going back to Godhead, back to home.

Bhagavad Gita Chapter 5, Text 26

Those who are free from anger and all material desires, who are self-realized, self-disciplined and constantly endeavouring for perfection, are assured of liberation in the Supreme in the very near future.

In verse 26, we see that kama, or unregulated desire, is seen as something to be avoided if one wants to achieve nirvana (liberation). Most boys would tend to think about intimacy with girls. However, they tend to think less about the pure soul animating the body of the girl, and more on the body itself. The Vedic understanding is that many of us can be a little mixed up. We like to have loving relations with real people, especially with a primary partner, but at times it's not pure love. We want to get something in return, whether for our ego, our mind or our body, in a multitude of subtle or obvious ways. This is kama. Many readers will be aware there is a text called the Kama-Sutra, and this is the same Sanskrit word we're referring to here. Sanskrit has various words for love, so kama can describe sensual romance or enjoyment of the senses, whereas prema (pronounced *pray'ma*) is pure love. As mentioned, our love tends to be mixed. We have a sense and desire that we want to have a purer love, but this is mixed up with more selfish desires:

"Well, what's in this for *me*?"

Gaudiya Vaishnava theology (Krishna consciousness) says that the constant and sincere meditation on Krishna, via the holy names in the mantra, is a primary way to get back on track. Srila Prabhupad, the founder of the modern Hare Krishna Society, says in his commentary to the Gita, verse 5.26:

"In the conditioned soul the desire to enjoy the fruitive results of work is so deep-rooted that it is very difficult even for the great sages to control such desires, despite great endeavours. A devotee of the Lord, constantly engaged in devotional service in Krishna consciousness, perfect in self-realization, very quickly attains liberation in the Supreme… He does not feel the pangs of material miseries; this state of life is called brahma-nirvāṇa, or the absence of material miseries due to being constantly immersed in the Supreme."

Despite an abundance of ancient wisdom, a young monk experiences hormones and memories churned up in a seductive soup, which can occasionally move to the forefront of his mind during meditation. Distraction in meditation means, for example, one is quietly chanting the Hare Krishna mantra - but mechanically - and the mind is drifting around the universe, looking for its version of happiness elsewhere.

There were times when this led to embarrassing situations. I wrote a poem about an incident when I lived on the island. A girl was passing through, staying in the ladies' part of the building for a week. She had flirtatious tendencies, and entertained herself by fluttering and smiling at the romance-starved boys in the temple. Here is the poem:

> An Exchange with a Guest
> All fluttery and taking advantage
> And attacking with sweet smiles
> Seeming to take a subordinate role
> While launching nice words in service
>
> After losing an exchange embarrassingly
> I retreated leaving grinning gaily
> Prowess shining through flicking banisters
> As I ascended to rest and reflect.
>
> Later armed with gravity,
> Philosophy and chanting internally
> I returned and exchanged more businessly
>
> Focusing on Krishna within the heart.

***

One day I was with 10 devotees, crossing the 200m of lake water in a rowing boat. We looked south towards Dernish Island and Crom and were alarmed to see a Biblical surge of water coming in our direction. The juvenile tsunami reached us quickly and we were tossed around, the oar snapped in two, and the boat was forced downstream, spinning out of control. The fierce winds fortunately brought the rowing boat ashore down the lake and we made our way through fields, woods and hedges back to familiar territory. Everyone was in good spirits with the excitement and thankful to Krishna that there were no injuries. Later we found out it was the tail end of a hurricane which had come across the Atlantic from the Caribbean.

***

One warm June evening, I was sitting out the front of Inish Rath house reading when I looked up to see a tall man dressed in black from head to toe walking ominously towards me and the temple building. As he approached an odour carried through the wind suggested he hadn't showered in weeks… or months. He announced to the world around him that he had come to stay.

"Where are my quarters?" he barked.

He had found a rowing boat on the mainland and rowed himself over. However, he gave off the aura of a troubled person. I didn't think he was a suitable person to stay.

Telling him I would return in a few minutes, I briskly walked around the building to talk to Aniruddha Das and others in case I might need help. Then I returned to deal with the daytime intruder. Although I believe in giving people a chance, in this case the man's attitude and presence gave a strong impression he wouldn't connect in our temple at that particular time.

"Do you know who I am?" he responded to me through dark, beady eyes. "No, but thank you for coming. However, we have no accommodation available at present," I said, praying to Krishna in the mind. I then carried on.

"I'm going to bring you back to the mainland now." The man in black was incensed. He towered over me fuming and I wondered if he'd pummel me. Fortunately, the daily meditations on the Hare Krishna mantra caught up with me and gave me some abhaya (fearlessness). I stood my ground. Then suddenly the atmosphere transformed. The man calmed, changed his attitude and peacefully agreed to depart. I rowed him back to the mainland and he walked away quietly, never to be seen again.

In July 1996 there was an Open Day on the island for members of the general public. For much of the 1990s Inish Rath Island had the nature of a private, insular retreat for ashram residents, which is non-standard for a temple of the International Society of Krishna Consciousness (ISKCON). However, on July the 20th 1996 five hundred local people wandered around the island listening to chant music, eating exotic food, enjoying the atmosphere, and small children jumped around wildly on a bouncy castle. Still fresh from the preaching frontlines some months before, I had strongly encouraged the idea to have the Open Day, and then Manu Das and Shyamananda Das did the actual work of setting up the event. The last Open Day had been eight years before. The back of the house was a mess, so I remember Shyamananda rushing around frantically. Just before visitors arrived he got some volunteers to help him erect an enormous colourful tarpaulin across two outdoor pillars, which functioned to prevent people from wandering into the dilapidated area.

The covering worked, and guests didn't get to see the mess at the back. In general, the whole day was a great success with hundreds of people enjoying festivities on the island – although just a few hundred visitors, as compared with a few thousand in 1986. Still we had less residents helping as compared to years before.

***

Hungary

In the late summer I travelled on three buses and two ferry boats, to Dublin, then London and then onto Hungary for the grand opening of the principal temple there. Due to governmental restrictions, Krishna consciousness in Eastern Europe had been slower to develop in the 1970s and '80s. However, in the 1990s temples were appearing all over the place from the plains of Hungary to the Baltic Sea, and from Siberia to the Black Sea.

In the early 1990s the then government in Hungary was so impressed with the sincere intentions of the Krishna devotees that they wanted to gift them several hundred hectares of land to develop a farm community. Sivarama Swami and the leadership had the foresight to realise that governments come and go, and future administrations may not be so favourable, so they preferred instead to purchase the land themselves at a very low price. Their foresight proved useful as a future national administration had a very different perspective of the world. This farm community, Krishna Valley, has developed into a world leader in sustainability. All cooking and heating are done with wood they grow, a large herd of cows provide organic milk, and bulls pull ploughs that till the earth. The community grows vegetables, fruits and grains, and they don't connect to mains electricity, preferring a simpler lifestyle. I spent an inspirational few days there experiencing a successful Hare Krishna farm community in action.

On September 5th, we celebrated Krishna Janmashtami – the appearance day of Lord Krishna and the day of the official opening of the Krishna Valley temple. The temple building was purpose-built, with a clean, modern, simple design. Sivarama Swami had been studying engineering at university when he joined the temple in the early 1970s, so he used his engineering skills to design a temple altar with built-in hidden rail-tracks. When desired for a festival, the sacred Deity forms could be wheeled outdoors to a balcony that overlooked an area where thousands of people could gather to view the radiant statue-like forms of Radha and Krishna.

***

Annually, on the Krishna Janmashtami day, devotees fast all day and then at midnight a music meditation and a ceremony take place. The devotees are meant to eat lightly when they break the fast, generally around 12.30am. However, in Ireland our wild and rebellious disregard for convention had us cooking lavish and rich feasts with panir curry, fried pastries with cheese, cream cakes, sweet rice, and many other delicacies. The year before, and the year before that, I had gotten stuffed drunk with mountains of delicious eatables. Of course, a serious devotee or mature person wouldn't do such a thing, but this is a book about an inexperienced youth.

So, on that day in Hungary, after fasting all day and doing meditation after meditation, and attending lectures, ceremonies and prayers, I felt I was due a prize for bring a good boy. I stood in a long line outdoors, eagerly awaiting my just rewards. Eventually coming to the front of the queue, in the night-time darkness and dimly lit open space, I picked up a plate. Just as I did so someone ladled in a dollop of lukewarm mashed potato. I stood motionless and speechless for a moment, looking at the food. This resembled canteen prison food, or dinner available in a soup kitchen for hungry people. My false ego rebelled. I had travelled across Europe for a festival, but *this* was not festival cuisine. This was like what you would feed a serious spiritual practitioner who simply wanted to break a fast with a little nourishment to keep body and soul together. I hadn't wanted *that!* I wanted to enjoy a heavenly party, not practise austerity like an ancient skinny yogi. Present-day Western civilisation often raises and produces many overly pampered young people, and I offer myself as an example. A training period of several years either in an army or in a monastery would do us all a world of good. At that stage, I had been living in the temple for three years, so I guess I'm a particularly slow learner.

The day after Krishna Janmashtami is always the celebration of the birthday of the founder of the Hare Krishna movement; Srila Prabhupad had been born on that day in 1896. After my ego had somewhat calmed down, I had another day of events, music and lectures. Devotees gathered in the temple room for most of the day. The opulent temple room had marble-like ceramic tiles on the floor, the walls were hand-painted with richly coloured holy images, and the ceiling area had glass, open to the sky. In the four corners of the room were enormous masonry kachelofen wood-stoves. These keep the space cosy in the winter.

***

Sivarama Swami as a person is a grave, authoritative figure and an expert manager. He always seemed to be the boss of everyone, including people his own age, a natural leader. But one devotee came to this event who was *his* boss, or rather his older god-brother: Tamal Krishna Goswami. (TKG). TKG had been one of the first devotees to join the society back in the sixties; and he was also grave, authoritative and an expert manager. It was interesting to see SRS (Sivarama Swami's commonly-used abbreviation) having his own authority, when usually he acted in the role of a father, teacher, or boss to other Krishna followers in Europe. At many events in Europe he was often viewed as the most senior person – the one with the final say on any important decisions. But when TKG was visiting Hungary for this event, he was the honorary senior figure. He would even tease his younger god-brother, in the manner of older brothers everywhere. I had never seen anyone tease SRS for anything before. Incidentally, a godbrother and godsister were terms that have been used in this culture for a century. These are non-biological 'siblings' with the same spiritual father, i.e. guru.

***

That night the temple room was packed full with devotees. It was dark outside. Candles gave the only illumination; in fact, in the temple room itself a single candle on top of the harmonium provided simple illumination for four hundred people. Sivarama Swami sang my favourite tune slowly and meditatively, with absorption, which leaves one in a state of heightened attention, clarity and devotion. I began to feel ashamed by my egotistical desire to enjoy eating fine food the night before. I felt a new appreciation for the inner joy of hearing sacred sound surrounded by the warm glow of candlelight.

Gurus and Swamis

In Vedic culture since time immemorial, it has been considered essential for a spiritual aspirant to find his or her own guru, or teacher. A guru is a person with years of training and experience in the philosophy and culture of the tradition, who is also willing to help guide some students. Most gurus are older men, and, occasionally, some are women. In the International Society for Krishna Consciousness (ISKCON) there are over 100 official gurus.

A swami is a senior monk who has taken a vow to never marry. Traditionally, swamis could have been previously married, but in their fifties or sixties husband and wife would have amicably separated. This is not the same as a modern divorce, but rather an arrangement that reflects changing roles within a family. There would often be several older sons for the mother to go to live with. She would carry on with grandmotherly duties, while the grandfather returned to a monastery. Before marriage he had been trained as a brahmachari student monk, and later in life he might aspire towards becoming a swami. A wife may also go to a women-only ashram. This might occur if she has no grandchildren, or maybe living with her children is challenging and not working out. In more modern times the woman may have the option of becoming a preacher and lecturer, if she so desires

***

Many gurus are swamis, however not all gurus are swamis, and not all swamis are gurus. Some gurus are married men. It depends on the individual spiritual advancement of the teacher, and his choice as to whether he thinks he's ready to teach as a guru. And some swamis want to live as a renounced monk, but do not yet feel ready to take on students. Maybe they will in the future. It remains to be seen. Traditionally, (ref. Caitanya Caritamrita Madhya-lila 4.111) many gurus were married men; but in the present-day a majority would be monks (swamis).

Fake Gurus

Fake gurus are those that a discerning person watches out for. They are usually in pursuit of money, power, fame, followers, sex, or control. Or, all of the above. They are basically dishonest people – mostly men – who are accomplished at acting. They can spin all kinds of yarns that favour their plan for themselves. They may look all misty and attractive wearing nicely-pressed robes, but under their somewhat deceptive appearances may lie something totally different.

Swamis with Challenges

In the early days of Hare Krishna younger men could take the vow of sannyasa. This is a life-long vow that the monk will never marry. They did significant voluntary service. But, in time, they realised that their outward renunciation was not on the same level as their inner realisation. Some just apologised to fellow followers of this culture, got a job, got married, helped raise a family, and got on with their lives. Others were involved with more scandal, as some of them were gurus, and their followers were very disappointed that the person whom they thought was pure and spiritual was more like the rest of us than had been imagined. Overall, both individuals and the Krishna Society learned many lessons.

As the religion matures and develops over the decades, it's now much more difficult for a man to take this vow. They get monitored and tested severally over four to eight years before they are allowed to become a swami nowadays, and they usually should be over 50 years old.

***

I visited Hungary for a week, and then I returned to Ireland via buses and boats. I had been living as a student in the ashram for more than three years at this stage, and as I had attended many lectures on Vedic wisdom and culture, I was developing a desire to find a teacher for myself. In the culture, it is understood one must be patient to wait until Krishna reveals a guru (teacher) to the aspiring student, from within. So, one evening on the island I wrote a letter… to Krishna! At night I placed my carefully handwritten letter under the curtain of the main altar in the temple, and I left it at that.

A few days later I woke up around 3.30am. I had had a dream the night before. In my dream, I was travelling all around the universe in a special vehicle or *vimana* (a Sanskrit word for an airplane or spaceship), and the purpose of the travelling was to share love of God with everyone everywhere. Among others in that flying vehicle was Sivarama Swami, and I had this sense that he was my guru. I felt enlivened, refreshed. This seemed to me to be a spiritual dream of deep significance. Sometime later, by letter, I requested Sivarama Swami to be my guru. He agreed, also by letter. Decades have passed since then, and my spiritual progress has been going forth at the speed of a half-lame tortoise. It is a work in progress.

- Temple Altar – Inish Rath Island -

- Young monks in Dublin temple, 1997 -

5

1997:

Island Life

Life carried on as normal on the lake of isle of Inish Rath. People would pass through staying for a few days, months, or a year or two.

Some men had an idea that we shouldn't be flushing our urine down the toilet and wasting valuable minerals that could be composted and recycled into Nature, so all the men began to urinate into barrels. However, later in '97 the men who had this noble idea didn't actually get around to doing the composting, and then they all departed from the island to live elsewhere. In time their minerals started to smell, so I remember struggling alone with huge heavy barrels of urine slopping all over the place as I carried them out to the great outdoors. The organic chemicals in the urine had already begun chemical reactions leading to incredibly strong smells. I cursed, mumbled and muttered as urine brewing for six months slopped onto my hands. Ahh, communal living. It had its ups… and downs.

Why Do People Join Temples and Ashrams?

In the Bhagavad Gita (BG 7.16) four general motivations are mentioned. There are:

(1) Those people in distress and who do not want to suffer; (2) those who would like to enjoy wealth and the pleasures of life; (3) people who are inquisitive, and (4) sages and philosophers who are searching for spiritual wisdom. Within a year or two of joining an ashram I heard this verse mentioned in lectures. Initially, in relation to myself personally, I would have considered:

"Hmm, so I guess I'm a seeker, and am searching for wisdom."

If the topic came up over the years, I would have been thinking like this, but as the years and decades passed by I gradually came to a more humble admission:

'Well, to be honest, I had personal motivations'.

I really am not keen on suffering too much. I haven't smoked cigarettes, or consumed alcohol or drugs in my life, as I know they lead to suffering, and – well – I don't like experiencing pain. I don't tend to cause too much distress to others. I wonder whether the motivation for acting this way is because I am mindful of karma. If one causes pain, one gets pain – and I don't want this. So, perhaps in reality, I don't care *that* much about others. I am really in pursuit of personal happiness… for me.

There is another affliction which can impact almost everyone in the world, and its effect can be even more pronounced in countries with more material wealth: mental distress. People may join ashrams because they are suffering in their minds and they are looking for some relief. Whether one has just had a relationship break-up, or is feeling lonely, lost, stressed, depressed or challenged in the mind in some way, these are all motivations for leaving one's usual life and searching for the structure and guidance of a temple or monastic living arrangement.

Another desire is wealth. In my younger days, I used to think that this applied to individuals who join temples in countries with a lower average income than richer countries. In a temple, residents get food (great food) and shelter, and they might even find ways to earn money in an international society by meeting people from around the world and having various opportunities opened up. But, as the years go by – while still mindful of others – one embarks on a more inward journey. What is wealth? It's not the paper notes, gold bullion or numbers on a screen in isolation that has value, but rather what we can acquire with this wealth.

Initially, we may have fewer possessions if we join an ashram, but do we have motivations to get trained up and mentally prepared so that later on in life we can acquire benefits for ourselves? Maybe we were struggling in the mind before we joined the temple, but the discipline of ashram life helps us to get ourselves together, so that we're psychologically and emotionally capable of managing a business or improving some talent that ends up giving us significant money / power.

Remember, Jesus, Buddha and Krishna are teaching spiritual truths for the soul. But we act in opposition to their teachings if we seek out material wealth for ourselves. Bhagavad Gita 8.16 reminds us that whether we're enjoying ourselves celestially (while saying the occasional prayer), or we're down in the dumps – either way, we are in the material world; not the spiritual world. As Buddha pointed out, we will still be prone to suffering, until we rise up to the next level, whether one sees that as Nirvana, the Kingdom of God, or Krishna Prema – pure love. Point being, even someone who is rich, attractive and successful, still has to eventually deal with physical pain, loss, death and destruction.

The Story Continues...

On March 17th almost all the Hare Krishna devotees in Ireland took part in the St. Patrick's Day parade in Dublin. Randy Repass, our American-born temple recruit, had organised and built a 50-foot-long serpent demon figure, with a scary mouth that opened 8 feet wide. The plan was that some volunteers would be 'eaten' by the demon, but then rescued by someone dressed as Krishna, based on a story from an ancient text called the Srimad Bhagavatam. Unfortunately, there was not enough time to perform this drama due to a little technical hitch. A tall colourful cart built by an English devotee was also part of the procession and the cart's steering mechanism got jammed. This held up thousands of people on the entire parade for 15 minutes. After that fiasco, we weren't invited back again! Despite this trouble, the day itself went extremely well, with hundreds of thousands of people finding a little peace by hearing the chanting of mantras and seeing colourful people. It is a bit of a head-turner when a group of kirtaneers are moving down the street, surrounded by thousands of local people and tourists in celebration of the National Day of the patron saint of Ireland.

***

In the early spring time, Sivarama Swami came to visit the island. Nowadays this devotee only eats dairy products produced on ahimsa farms i.e. Hare Krishna or other farms that look after the cows with love, massages, and cuddles. They do some milking of the cows, but are very mother-and-calf orientated, and they never send the cows to be killed. However, at that time, he would eat any dairy products, like most Hare Krishna and also most Indian vegetarians do. One of the Hungarians who came with him told me "Sivarama Swami wants to eat karmi cheese," so asked could I have that added to the shopping list. 'Karmi' is like the Hare Krishna word for infidel or heathen, i.e. the non-believers. Not so many people use the term in that context any more. 'Karmi cheese' here refers to a block of cheddar from a shop. In temples, we hardly ever ate things made outside, and never cooked grains or beans. So 'karmi cheese' seemed like a slight indulgence. In later life former monks will relax on the rules, but when devotees are in strict ashram consciousness they are very careful as to what they put into their mouths and bodies. Anything made in a factory by a for-profit company is looked down upon. One prefers to eat temple food, or homemade food that is cooked from carefully selected raw ingredients in a spiritual home.

The next morning everyone was doing japa meditation in the temple room, when swami looked around and asked, "Where are all the ladies?" From 5.15am when japa began, all the ladies would leave the men to feel the energies of the temple room. Meanwhile, the fairer sex made do with practising their meditation in the dining room, in hallways or in ashram bedrooms. No one had thought about this point before. This had been introduced by European and American temple management systems years before, and everyone who came along just thought this was the done and accepted thing. Swami hinted that this wasn't really fair on the women. So he said, "Look, it's a long room... go and invite the ladies to come back in, and men can be on one side and women on the other." So the custom changed and to this day, that is what is done. Women, if they wish, join the men in the temple room during the personal meditation time.

***

After giving some lectures on the island, I caught a lift in swami's van as he was going to Dublin to visit the temple there. It was Saturday afternoon, and we drove through Cavan town. Swami asked a young English devotee and myself to go out and sell books while he had some service to attend to for an hour. He commented that someone has to pay for the petrol, so rather than us hanging around, we could contribute.

So there and then we were given a few books and sent out to face the general public. My collection came to about £8.20. The English boy was on fire with enthusiasm – he sold six or seven times more books than I did. I appreciated the parental 'guru' lessons from the swami: "Don't be idle" and "Earn your keep". We should endeavour to contribute and give back to our communities and families.

The temple in Dublin had moved to a rented building on South William Street. There was a jam-packed Sunday Feast event, and the lecture was electric. At the questions and answers time, one woman who had lived in another temple years before, indicated that she had experienced some type of improper or unfair treatment from whoever was in charge at that time. You could hear a pin drop with the tension as everyone waited with baited breath to see how swami would respond. 90% of the people in the room were not Hare Krishna followers, but the general Irish public.

"How on earth will he get out of this one?" I thought to myself.

The swami responded with firmness, gentleness and compassion, and asked the woman how she saw Krishna in all of this. It really emerged that she wasn't attributing blame to Krishna for what had happened before. These were individuals who had behaved poorly, but she could not bring herself to blame Krishna. I felt she was satisfied with the response.

After the lecture swami wanted to get some fresh air, so he asked me to accompany him, and soon we found ourselves wandering down Grafton Street. From the bottom of Grafton Street to the top – all 500m long – on three occasions we were politely stopped by passers-by and different people had questions of a philosophical and theological nature for swami. This was an example of why it is a service to others to wear the robes of a monk. If we had been wearing trousers and jerseys, no one would have stopped us. At the shop Habitat, swami bought some metal candle lanterns for the Hungarian farm, where they use many candles as they don't have mains electricity.

***

While these events were happening in Ireland, our Head Monk, Tribhuvanatha Das, had started to bring Irish and English young men, and a few women, to various countries in Africa to help him host Hare Krishna festivals. I heard stories that they would sometimes arrive with a van-load of devotees in some small or medium sized town, and immediately begin singing and chanting on the streets with drums and cymbals. Africans would just stop what they were doing and come and join in the singing and chanting – literally most people in the town. Africans really got into the rhythm, and danced with pure joy easily visible on their faces.

One time, Tribhuvanatha and a British Indian devotee were walking in a city when they became aware that they were being followed. Five men were approaching quickly and it seemed obvious that they were going to attack. As the two Hare Krishnas had long flowing robes, Tribhuvanatha formulated a plan. Though just 5 foot 6 inches (1.66m) tall himself, he performed an *act*. He began making ninja warrior karate moves and sounds, slashing the air with his hands, judo kicks, and whatever other Eastern warrior moves he could think of. The other devotee followed his lead, both looking as intimidating as possible. Somehow… it worked! The five men slunk away into an alley way, never to be seen again.

***

On another occasion, four car-loads of devotees were driving hundreds of miles from one city to another in Uganda. They had to sleep overnight in the cars out in the middle of nowhere. It was stifling hot, even at night, and most of the men slept on the bonnets of the cars or on yoga mats outside, to try to catch whatever slightly cooling breeze was available.

The next morning, as they were gathering themselves together and preparing to move off, some armed rangers approached them. These are the men whose job it is to protect rhinos and elephants from getting shot by poachers. When the rangers heard where the devotees slept that night, they laughed. They informed them they were lucky they didn't get eaten by lions or hyenas!

***

In India the previous year, I had bought a range of supplies to equip new recruits with chanting beads, neck beads, dhoti robes, Indian herbal toothpaste and other items. Between 1992 and 1995 about 20 young Irish people had joined the temples, so I had just assumed they would carry on joining up. However, in retrospect, it seems that people are more likely to join temples when there is a senior inspirational teacher who has purity and / or charisma, or when the Society is especially well organised with good facilities (which was not the case with ISKCON Ireland). In the last festival that Tribhuvanatha hosted in Ireland, a young man addressed the crowd during Q&A time. He gave his doubts about 'organised religions'. Tribhuvanatha smiled warmly at him saying: "You should join us, we're *really* not organised!" He was referring to the International Society for Krishna Consciousness in Ireland.

Another motivating factor for people to transform their lives and move into a temple was seen in Eastern Europe. Here there had been severe restrictions on freedom for decades, and then as people were suddenly free to choose, tens of thousands of people joined new temples and ashrams in those regions.

If any of the aforementioned elements are not in place then people don't often have an impetus to give up their lives and join an ashram. Young people are also attracted to join where there is already a group of young people in that ashram. Hare Krishna as a religion specialises in attracting 18- to 25-year-olds, whereas many hatha yoga ashrams would attract older people. Part of the reason for this may be connected with the fact that Krishna consciousness demands a more complete change of culture, which is an easier thing to do when one is younger.

From 1996 onwards, Tribhuvanatha Das had begun sharing wisdom and spiritual music in Great Britain and in several African countries, and consequently was spending less time in Ireland. His leadership had been so subtle and low-key that we hadn't even noticed that his presence and guidance had been an enormous motivating factor for us to join and serve in the temple. In India I had bought devotional clothes and mantra beads for new recruits, but these things just ended up as stock for the temple shop because hardly any young people joined after 1996.

***

Over the summer my mother kindly bought me a gift of a rowing boat. However, as monks don't own significant personal possessions, the boat immediately became the main temple rowing boat for the next five years. Monks have their own clothes, books, chanting beads, toothbrushes, and tape cassettes for listening to lectures. They tend not to have much else.

Listening to kirtan sacred music and lectures on the philosophy and theology is considered important for a monk and a seriously practising devotee. Therefore machines that play sound like tape cassette players were used frequently. It's common for these machines to also have a built-in radio; however no one in the temple would ever play the radio. It wouldn't even cross the mind to want to listen anything regarded as being "non-devotional". To sully the sacrosanct airwaves inside the temple space with material sound vibration just wasn't going to happen. Except one day on September 1st 1997, Shyamananda somehow got to hear that Princess Diana had just died. Maybe someone was out that morning in a local shop and saw a newspaper headline? I don't know. But, he couldn't help but want to hear the news, so he sneaked away to the office, locked the door, and was listening to the BBC as others were out chopping wood or doing other services. I think he wanted to connect with the emotional experience of tens of millions of people in shock. It was the only time that I was aware of that anyone ever listened to the radio in the temple. Nowadays, with mobile phones and the internet, ashram residents are more likely to be connected to news; but before these machines came along, we really switched off. We were early converts to the *Digital Detox*.

***

One silent, eerie night in November '97 I heard a panicked series of shrill screams coming from the lake. My heart raced as I rushed out to investigate. I sprinted down through a cold mist, desperate to discover the cause of the screaming. Mandy, now Kalyani Devi Dasi, had been coming over in the rowing boat but had gotten stuck, and her screams indicated she was in immediate danger. It was bitterly cold out there and something was holding on to the boat. Luckily, Randy Repass – now living on the mainland – had his own canoe. He launched it and furiously paddled out to rescue Mandy. The cause of the problem was that a metal chain on the boat had been left dragging in the water and this had become entangled in dying lake vegetation. The boat had then tilted to one side, threatening to tip Mandy into the freezing water. The lake can be dangerous. On Friday December 29th 1961 a local postman, William Rooney, was on his way home to his wife and family when his rowing boat got caught in ice due to abnormally severe weather. His brother James went to his assistance as darkness began to descend, but his boat also got stuck. Tragically the two brothers were found the next day, frozen to death, close to each other. Mandy was more fortunate. Randy managed to untangle the rowboat and get her safely over to the island.

∗∗∗

Another night I returned from the mainland and walked up the dark wooded path. The front door creaked as I entered the 12-bedroomed Victorian country house. On turning into the hallway corner a white-faced seated Mandy startled me. "You look like you've seen a ghost," I said. She stared silently; her eyes and body language spoke. In time she opened her mouth to speak. Early in the night she had heard thudding footsteps coming towards the room she was staying in, but each time she opened the door to see who was there, the corridor was devoid of any signs of life. And then inside the bedroom an empty plastic water bottle started sucking itself in and out of its own accord. Mandy barely slept that night.

In the Vedic worldview a person can sometimes enter the body of a bhuta (ghost) due to his or her karma. It's a temporary situation meant for the education of the soul. The soul in the subtle body of the bhuta has the desires of a person with a body, but cannot fulfil those desires. The bhuta still has the same mind of the person he or she was in his past life, and sometimes the mind's desires or frustrations can have an effect on dull matter. This had been my understanding from shastra (the ancient texts) and the Vedic worldview, but it was fascinating to see shastra come to life… in a sense.

It seems there was a subtle entity floating through the corridors of Inish Rath House in 1997, as I also had my own experience. The boys out in the van came back to the temple for a spiritual break, after distributing books to members of the public. Eight of us were sprawled out in a room: sleeping bags and camping mats; boys' clothes, tape cassette players, robes, toothpaste, and other items strewn all over the place. It was around 1.00am when I had an experience of some entity subtly weighing me down. Many people will say that this was a figment of my imagination, but in my life I've never yet been drunk, intoxicated, psychotic, depressed or suicidal and I'm confident I can distinguish between another entity (person) and my imagination. I've never before or since had such an experience. I wanted the 'presence' to leave, but it would not. Within my mind I went to remember the holy name of Krishna; however the entity was blocking and preventing me bringing the holy name to the level of the mind. I had to try and try with a massive effort, and eventually I broke through – so to speak – in my mind and I shouted "Krishna!" At that very moment I subtly felt an enormous weight lifting off me, and the presence was gone. Some people might think I'm fooling myself. They can believe as they like, but I know I wasn't *imagining* anyone there: there was a soul in a subtle body that had a potentially negative outlook towards me. I couldn't see this with my eyes but, well, we don't actually see *any* mental thing using light waves travelling to the retinas of our eyes. The mind can construct images, but in this case, I wasn't even seeing anything in the mind. It was a real experience: a strong feeling of a presence. As it wasn't experienced through the senses one begins to get stuck for words to describe the incident. For me, it was fascinating. There is a term Mind-Body-Soul, and I feel I actually experienced these three levels of existence that night. My physical body was hardly involved, but a struggle took place on the level of the mind, and myself, a soul, had to remember the name of Krishna and fight to bring this holy name to the mental plane.

***

Inish Rath House is an imposing 19th century country house with tall ceilings. We often didn't have enough money to heat the place during quiet times when the house was empty, and I was sometimes in the main men's ashram room on my own. I'm not exaggerating to say there were times when I slept overnight in the winter with three duvets, a hat, a scarf, a tee-shirt, a jersey, a coat, long-johns, tracksuit bottoms, and two pairs of socks, trying to keep warm in a room that was three degrees Celsius. Only a sliver of my face was peeping out: the area that needs the air… and fresh cool air it was. Thankfully, things have improved since then.

***

One cool evening I went outdoors to get some fresh air. It was a cloudless night. Inish Rath House is located in an open space at the centre of the island, surrounded in all directions by mature woodlands. The sky above was vast, open, star-speckled and with a half moon.

I stood with my body arched backwards and with eyes gazing up to the heavens in a kind of visual meditation. In a rural area with no light pollution there are times when one is treated to these scenes, if only we take the time to be present in the moment.

"There is The Plough… There is Orion" I thought.

My reverie was broken by movement. A light – which appeared to be a star – was moving across the sky. It made haphazard and random movements, progressing in one direction slowly and then tracing an arbitrary circle. It then moved off in some other direction at a different speed. This went on for several minutes. I gazed into the sky with fascination, observing and monitoring this little light. My mind raced: was it an airplane, a helicopter, or a torch? A torch would cast a beam of light across the sky, but there was no such beam. The movements were too erratic and fast at times to be a helicopter or airplane, and besides the night sky was quiet and silent. I do not know what that light was, but in my mind, I couldn't see any evidence that it had an easily explainable man-made source. For me, this was exciting. A few months before I had read a book called *Alien Identities* written by a scientist and mathematician who had later become a Hare Krishna devotee. I had been an avid reader of science fiction as a boy. Alien Identities talked about life on other planets in the universe, as discussed in the ancient Vedic texts. And here I was, standing outdoors star-gazing and seeing an unexplainable flying object. I still do not know what I saw that night. Some people might think that my mind was projecting some fantasy, or hallucinating. But I do not think so. I'd like to be able to conclude and explain what I saw, but I can't. I do now know what I saw. I guess it wasn't that exciting. I mean, nothing landed and beamed me up to the Mothership. I didn't have oval-headed humanoids performing experiments on my body. But then, I wouldn't be too keen on experiencing this anyway, thank God.

- Inish Rath House -

- Janaki -

6

1998:

Grace

In Northern Ireland the peace process really began developing from 1998 as decades of Troubles entered the annals of history. Hostile parties were left with tension and memories, but at least the conflict had calmed down enough so that the streets of towns started to look like they had rejoined contemporary Europe. This change saw tourism returning to Northern Ireland. Once, when I was a boy in the '80s, we went to Belfast on the train for shopping. Food and many consumer items were cheaper in the North. I remember seeing armoured cars, British army patrols, bomb units, checkpoints and street barriers. To a nine-year-old boy it resembled a scene from a war film.

But now, commemorative statues promoting peace were being commissioned; and tourists from Germany, Austria and Switzerland were hiring cruiser boats to explore what Tourism Ireland promoted as the longest navigable lake-river system in Europe, the Shannon-Erne Waterway.

I enrolled in a tourism course promoted by a government-funded agency to assist business start-ups. Their offices were just outside the county town. A rowing boat, a bicycle ride, a bus journey and a two mile walk in my sandals got me there.

Manu Das and I had some tourism ideas for Inish Rath Island, and my mother kindly came from Dublin and drove me around several visitors' centres so I could get a feel for the industry. Manu generously raised the money for the required infrastructure and facilities like the refurbishment of the approach road, the repair of the temple's 18 tonne metal barge which had been out of service for 9 years), and an upgrade of kitchen and dining facilities. We were preparing to open up the temple for tourists.

∗∗∗

One bright April morning after meditations, prayers and the first meal, the temple's phone rang and I answered it. An enchanting voice interrupted my day. It was a girl sounding sunny and endearing, with a 'down under' vibe. I gave directions, and she came to stay for a few days. It turned out she had stayed in a temple ashram in New Zealand before. The next morning, I rounded a bend in the hallway, and Grace was standing there washing her plate after breakfast. I stood pretending to look blankly at a wall, waiting, as if I was unattached to the world around me. The clock tick-tocked in the kitchen and the sun unfurled, lighting up the high-ceilinged pantry of the Victorian house. A cobweb appeared in the sunlight. "I can wash your plate." Grace swivelled around flashing a delightful service smile. My romance-less youth was suddenly overcome by flowery feminine loveliness as I stood there, orange robed, while inside I recoiled from attraction versus aversion dilemmas. Conflicting thoughts raced through my mind.

"Student monks don't chat to girls."

"But she's so lovely."

"Women are a distraction for monks."

"She looks and sounds like an angel."

"I want to marry her."

"Stop, you're being ridiculous."

I politely responded to the girl, grateful for her kindness. Later on I found myself showing her the rowing boat to paint; it required some attention after a winter's battering by the elements. There were the two of us down by a sun-dappled old log quay and forest clearing at the lakeshore; expansive sky, lapping water and fresh moving air on the skin; streams of life energy, wide open nature refreshing the senses.

Vilnis, the Latvian, came and helped us drag the boat onto land then he carried on back up the track to the temple building. I got chatting with Grace about some recent news:

Devotees of the London Soho Street temple had appeared a few weeks prior to this in adverts all over the city's underground rail system sitting meditatively, saffron-robed in *padmasana* (sitting cross-legged) with a clever slogan advertising something or other. We both thought this was exciting, if funny, exposure for Hare Krishna.

Later on my service was to clean the main sections of the temple but I was also doing some paperwork - applying for a tourism grant for European funds allocated to the border regions of Ireland. The closing date was approaching quickly so I really wanted to use the rowing boat and bicycle to get myself to the post office to send the applications straight away. Grace stayed to clean and when I returned from the mainland she was still scrubbing away on the floor, knees to the ceramic tiles, just as one is meant to clean in a temple, traditionally. She looked up with a feline-like arch and smiled amiably, and I was just so impressed – she looked so pretty. I was in love!

I was a 23-year-old, man acting like a 16-year-old boy, with the added complication that I was a monk. For the humour element, I'll tell you the story.

Although it is acknowledged that most student monks will marry and get jobs when they are in their late twenties or in their thirties, during the time they are monks they're not supposed make direct plans for this, and they're certainly not meant to be chatting to the girls about anything other a minimum of words about temple service – briefly – in a public place.

Grace worked in the new visitors' centre at Newgrange[3] and she suggested in a letter that someone from the temple could come for a free tour, seeing as though we wanted to open a visitors' centre also. So, on the sort of clear and bright summer day that makes us all believe this is how it will always be... I arrived.

I was side-glancing at the foreign car registrations. As I walked up the clean paving, American, French, German and Japanese tourists added cosmopolitan glamour which complimented the free summery sky feeling of the day.

Entering the visitors' centre was like stepping into the hive of a busy airport, except the stone tiles and natural décor created more earthly energies here. After several hours, the day had gone really well but I also had a secret mission. Heart thumping in a frozen moment amid the foyer bustle I handed

---

[3] *Newgrange is a circular 80m-diameter building built of eternal stone and covered with a green dome of grass. Radiocarbon dating of the main doorway remains suggests construction at around 3,200 BC. It is situated 30 miles (50 km) north of Dublin. Incidentally, 3200BC is also close to the time when Krishna was active and teaching in ancient India. The date for Krishna's presence comes to human society from the position of the stars in the heavens. A section of the Vedas deals with astronomy. If one enters the positions of heavenly bodies given for that time into a modern astronomy programme, the date for the speaking of Bhagavad Gita is 3,067 BC.*

Grace a stiff envelope containing a letter. "This is from me," I said, and then I left.

Four days later there was a big festival at the island temple of Inish Rath. There was also a wedding, Hindu-style. What we call in Ireland a heat-wave – a week of unusually warm, sunny weather – was gracing the countryside, and all the trees and grasses were happy and flourishing. Early that morning just after 4.30, I had glanced around the temple room to see the space jam-packed full of pilgrims swaying from side to side, and erupting in esoteric ecstasy. I was singing like a Welshman on the top of a mountain, delighted to be sharing the moment with more of a crowd than the usual few residents.

After breakfast, men were erecting a marquee, their spirits lifted in the sunshine. People were arriving, carting around their luggage. One could hear drumbeats from the temple inside as subtle rhythms reverberated through the walls. Children were laughing, someone was looking flustered over something, and old friends were meeting… it was all going on. The whole place was alive and buzzing with activity. Lectures, kirtan music, and then the wedding ceremony began. Every now and again I would catch a glimpse of Grace through the crowd, "What would happen?" I thought. "How would she respond to my letter?"

Wedding guests shove-rubbed and jostled against each other in the hallway of the Victorian house that wasn't designed for so many, and the celebration social vehicle was manoeuvring around. A sea of faces filled my view so that crossing 20 feet seemed like a huge undertaking. At one point I slumped down in the stairs cradling my chin and looking perplexed. Monkhood or romance? One or the other? A Wexford man noticed this shy, robed boy and put his hand on my shoulder, massaging it firmly. "Cheer up son, it's not so bad," he said. It all seemed like a drama. He didn't even know what my problem was, but perhaps he guessed the general issue.

It's a little sad when everyone begins to leave. I experienced people chanting and singing together, feasting, associating, chatting, laughing – as though the festival would go on forever. But then groups of people begin to depart, leaving empty spaces; used rooms with scattered things... a heavy-laden quiet descended on the Victorian mansion with its creaky floor-boards and old wood.

***

I ended up rowing Grace and three strangers back to the mainland after the festival. On the 19th-century stone quay, the others went on ahead and Grace turned and our eyes met for the first time that day. I was nervous like a love-struck teenager. She politely mentioned that she'd reply to my letter soon. My eyes were sparkling, excited with the whole thing. Back on the island guests were leaving in droves, and then even the normal residents also left. I was practically on my own.

The contrast from a buzzing celebration to a remote, desolate island was stark. Tables, chairs, rubbish, sound equipment and a thousand random items were strewn all over the place. It took me three days on my own to get everything back in order.A letter came in the post a few days later. Grace communicated in a gentle way, writing with remarkably clear and balanced handwriting. She said she had come to Ireland to get some space after some personal challenges, but her flight back to New Zealand was in five days. She said she wasn't ready for a husband yet.

In traditional Hare Krishna and Vedic culture a man is either a monk or a married man. I couldn't really think of an in between. I had mentioned to her in my letter that she was very nice, and asked would she be interested in chatting about getting married in the future. At this stage I was still a young man with very little life experience, and even less romantic experience. Years have passed since these juvenile romantic incidents, and I only remember the details because I wrote about them at that time. Grace hadn't acted inappropriately… any fault was mine. The challenge that comes up is that rather than seeing her as a person and a soul, I was getting distracted by the physical outward covering. In this consciousness, one becomes impersonal and sees another person as an object which might bring us happiness through the senses, the emotions or false ego.

Now a monk isn't supposed to be sending private letters to girls, but then one is hard-pressed to find everything perfect in this world. Rowing across the lake later on that day in a gale, and cycling seven miles to make the Speed Post deadline in a local post office I rushed to send Grace a concluding letter wishing her well before she returned to the far side of the world. I reminded myself, even as I cycled, of a particular 1980s TV advert where a James Bond-like man conquers mountains, parachutes down and then battles the raging elements just so he can enjoy a *liaison* with a lady friend. He presents to her – in this case – a very special purple box of chocolates. I wondered should I include this story in the book, as it exposes me as being foolish. But, rather than criticise others, I chose to offer myself as an example. At times, men can be outrageously mesmerised by the opposite sex, as discussed in the Srimad Bhavavatam in numerous parables. Some examples are Canto 4 Chapter 25; Canto 6 Chapter 1; Canto 8 Chapters 8 to 12; Canto 9 Chapter 14; and Canto 9 Chapter 20. Below please note Canto 4, Chapter 25, Texts 20 –25.

"While wandering here and there in that wonderful garden, King Puranjana suddenly came into contact with a beautiful woman who was walking there without any engagement. She was very beautiful and young, and she appeared anxious to find a suitable husband. The waist and hips of the girl were gorgeous. She was dressed in a yellow sari with a golden belt. While she walked, her ankle bells rang. She appeared exactly like a denizen of the heavenly regions. With the end of her sari, the woman was trying to cover her breasts, which were equally round and well placed side by side. She again and again tried to cover them out of shyness… Puranjana, the hero, became attracted by the eyebrows and smiling face of this demigoddess."

***

In Canto 8 God Himself, who appears as multiple avatars throughout human history, appears in a female form called Mohini-Murti. The devas (demigods) and asuras (demons) are engaged in conflict, and Mohini wanders onto the scene, and Her beauty is so otherworldly and striking that She bewilders the minds of the demons. Later on, the primary demigod of them all, who missed what had transpired earlier on, was curious to see God in a female form. He went to the Lord's abode, and the Lord agreed to show him this form. Shiva is the master of all yogis and ascetics. He can't be affected by ordinary lust. However when Mohini arrived, She displayed the full extent of Her bewildering energy, and Shiva became mad with desire. This story is seen as an example of God arranging a situation in order to give instruction to humanity and enjoy some interactions with His avatars or devotees. Even if one attains great heights in society like becoming a swami or a senior yogi on the level of samadhi, one should always remember that even Lord Shiva – who invented Yoga – could apparently become attracted to, distracted and mesmerised by feminine charm.

Someone might comment that it's natural for boys and girls to be attracted to each other, and if this assists with the continuation of the species, what is the problem? This point is true. Here we're talking about where one's good sense becomes overcome. One can begin to objectify the boy or girl, and see them as some*thing* that we try to use for selfish desire. Maybe my ego likes to be married to a super model? Someone pleasing to the eye, someone who I will get something out of for **me**. Whatever it is, one wants to learn to love and to give, not to take and exploit.

***

In the pursuit of happiness I might have been spoiled for choice, whether as a budding romantic, or as an Eastern monastic. I also experienced many moments of deep satisfaction living in the temple. One of the primary texts of the East, Bhagavad Gita, is profound and expansive. Henry David Thoreau, the 19th century American philosopher and writer, said:

"In the morning, I bathe my intellect in the stupendous and cosmogonal philosophy of the *Bhagvat Geeta;* since whose composition years of the gods have elapsed, and in comparison with which our modern world and its literature seem puny and trivial."

There is a certain satisfaction that comes with attending the early morning meditations for years, and then just sharing philosophical wisdom with groups of people who visited the temple every now and again. These included local people, groups from the Share Holiday Village nearby, or Indian families. It brought me joy to do this simple service for the benefit of others. We often had various youth and community groups visiting. I remember a sense of calm and peace as I sat looking into the eyes of people, and we would discuss ancient Vedic explanations for life, the universe and everything.

My Understanding of some Vedic Teachings

For those who may not be interested, the next section is my understanding of some of the Vedic teachings. We get back to the story when I talk about a new 'tourist venture'.

***

Veda, with millions of Sanskrit words, gives an indication it has a fair idea of what's going on. A fundamental idea is **we are not this body**. Because we think we are, that is the root cause of suffering. In Bhagavad Gita18.61 Krishna compares the body to a *yantra*, or machine, or in other words, a vehicle for carrying the soul around. In BG 7.4 and 7.5 Krishna makes a distinction between matter, and the spirit-soul – the jiva (pronounced 'jeeva' with first syllable as in jeep).

Soul is our identity, who we are. Everything else changes, but my identity as being *me* remains. I am always an individual soul. Whether a thousand years in the past, or in the future, I am still **me**. My body changes, my mentality changes, but I still have my own identity. Just as we might have a memory from when we were aged four. Since then, all the living cells in our body have been replaced and our way of thinking, desires and ambitions have changed. The only thing that is constant is that I know that was me being woken up in the dark by my mother to prepare to go to see Pope John Paul II in 1979. I remember thinking at the time, "Wow, we're getting up in the middle of the night," (it was the early morning). Bodily identification is the cause of both our physical suffering and our social squabbling. Our bodies are designed such that they are constantly decaying, and there is a point where one eventually just has to get a new one. In relation to challenges between people, there is a general tendency to form ourselves into groups based on where our body is from, what colour it is, what religion it is assigned to, or whatever other classification or category we can come up with or identify with.

So we have: Catholics, Protestants; blacks, whites; East End, West End; northerners, southerners; sun tribe, moon tribe, and so on. According to Veda, a soul has his own form, home and purpose but sometime in the distant past we made a choice to strike out alone and explore the world of matter, neglecting our own true selves.

Someone who doesn't intellectually believe that Krishna exists might argue that that this Krishna isn't very nice as why, for example, does he allow bone cancer in little children? Veda responds thus:

"The material world isn't our real home. By nature, it is a place where there is violence, suffering, decay, and disease."

In Gaudiya Vaishnava theology Krishna was happy, lovingly embracing us in the spiritual world but He also doesn't stand in the way of our free choice. With reincarnation, a five-year-old child today could have been an 84-year-old man a few years before. By coming to the material world, we became involved in karma. Karma is the universal reaction to our activities. When we paid for a well to get dug out in a famine-area village in 1985 we got some good karma; however, when we ate that beef sandwich on August the 8th 1991, we became implicated in karma of the not so good variety. When a particular Friesian cow got held up by her hind legs on July 24th of that year and experienced excruciating pain and an unimaginable terror Veda teaches that some karma will be due to anyone involved, whether the killer, purchaser or eater.

Karma is carried from lifetime to lifetime. Is this nice? No. Is a child getting bone cancer nice? No. Is a baby duckling being swallowed whole by a pelican nice? No. Is a baby lion cub being bitten on the throat and killed by another male lion nice? No.

The explanation of Veda is that the material world has some beautiful features like lush forests, rainbows and sunrises; however, there is also violence and suffering. That is Material Nature.

Beautiful features are a replica of what is found in the Spiritual World. However, violence and suffering are unique to this Material World. When someone questions why Krishna allows bone cancer in little children they are making some assumptions that the person is their body (i.e. "**I am** this physical body"), they are not the soul, and that reincarnation and karma do not exist. In our own observation, reincarnation takes place. I can observe my identity as me remains the same, but my body changes all the time. Gradually, but consistently, we see our bodies change in size and in age: reincarnation – getting a different body – even in this one lifetime.

When one examines the materialistic philosophy in detail one discovers that they believe "**I am** this body." I should be civil to others, which is fine, but I should also try to enjoy life just with this body and mind (Veda says this is not complete).

Veda questions this philosophy. Some people don't agree. They'll take it that having Krishna as the supreme architect and designer sounds like a fairy story. But we can only accept and respect that various viewpoints exist. Some may argue that there is no architect and no designer - that our bodies and the world around us are accidental. If one is wandering in the jungle for hours, and then comes across an ancient temple with stone carvings, one would automatically assume that some people created this in the past. One doesn't know who, just that someone (or some people) did it. Similarly, my own body is a much more complex system than that ancient temple, either now, or when the place was in its heyday. One may not know yet who created the bodies, but one can assume it was somebody.

Some people say, "That's okay, but **no one** can know who the intelligent source is."

One response to this is: "***You*** do not know everybody. You may not know something now, or yet, but you can't speak for billions of other people. Just because *you* don't know God, doesn't mean that someone else doesn't know Him, or Her."

I know plenty of people who see the world in the Vedic way. They don't have faith in the view that the universe popped out of either nothingness, or from an infinitesimal point, and that subsequently matter exploded and – over time – formed a horse, a peacock and you and me. In material philosophy, accidents, chance and inert matter are the fundamental causes of complex life.

My own body is so much more complex than my car or my computer. If one gave nature four billion years, do you think it could throw together a computer?

Maybe Mother Nature could get someone to pop over to the Middle East to extract some petroleum, and then ship a consignment of this off to China to process and create some plastic. Simultaneously, a few volunteers might head off to the Congo to mine some minerals, and finally someone with intelligence needs to combine everything together to create a useful machine. We're hard-pressed to imagine that nature can throw together a Porsche car or an Apple computer using any amount of flooding, lightening, hurricanes, volcanoes and mudslides, in any amount of time.

Nature tends to decay complex systems over time, not create them; like an intelligent being can create a car, but time and nature will rust the metal and eventually return the car to a simpler system. Veda's viewpoint is that the life-force in living things is spiritual and that matter – the physical body – is only temporarily animated due to the presence of spirit.

So, in the example above, it appears an intelligent being (or beings) is required to create a complex form like the body of a human. In Veda, this creator is a person called Krishna. Krishna is the ultimate CEO, but He works through avatars like Vishnu, or demigods like Shiva and Shakti. Veda sees there is one God, but there are also agents of God who assist with the running of the material world (demigods / powerful sages / angels). The agnostic scientific worldview sees these as nice stories for entertainment. The Veda has a different worldview. Mother Nature is Shakti, the wife of Shiva. Veda respects Nature as a 'she'. Modern secular science identifies Nature as an 'it'. Modern secular science believes that inert matter is the fundamental source, and everything either comes from nothing, or from a little point of condensed **stuff** that definitely is not a person.

***

Tourist Venture

In 1998 we started guided tours of the temple as a tourist venture, which shared the culture of the tradition, but also to generate some much needed income for the house and grounds. We also got a computer. I'd say it's very likely someone donated it, as the temple would never have had have a budget for a machine like that. I came to hear about email for the first time. There was also something called www.something-or-other.com, but I hadn't figured out what that was yet. Hare Krishna temples around the world had some internal email system where one could send a message to every temple participating. This was our main use of the computer. I didn't know that there were other email systems other than the internal Krishna one, and I hadn't heard about internet search yet. We received an email that a devotee from Canada was travelling around Europe and a warning that he shouldn't be allowed to stay in any temple. I looked at the name mentioned. "Hold on, that's the man who stayed here with his family a few weeks ago," I thought as I read the message.

I read on. He was abusive to his wife and two step-daughters, physically beating them. The girls were older teenagers. This was definitely the same man. I was in shock. As he had *seemed* so nice I had even asked him to take a few guided tours and talk to groups of temple visitors. This was an unfortunate surprise. To think that some people can wear robes and act like they are nice, when really something more sinister is going on.

***

Manu Das purchased a 20-foot former fishing boat with a flat bottom and a partial roof-cover to assist in getting visitors to the island. I remember a well-to-do-looking young couple arrived one day. I drove the boat over, but the propeller stopped revolving due to getting stuck in reeds and lake vegetation. The couple waited only seven metres away, but the boat wouldn't budge. Such was my desire for these people to visit the temple for the arati, or scheduled ancient ceremony, that I jumped into the water, robes and all. I scrambled to free the vegetation as quickly as possible, all the time assuring them that everything was fine. I remember the bemused look on their faces as they politely tried to weigh up if they really wanted to come with me in that boat. Temple residents are servants of the general public, and are meant to have no expectation that the public give them anything in return. So, dripping wet, I guided them up to the temple, and made sure they were seen to first, and then I put on fresh, dry robes. Head Monk Tribhuvanatha Das had given an example of how to serve. Not that one wants to 'enjoy' the satisfaction; however there is a wonderful sense of fulfilment when one learns to just serve others and not want anything from them. You're not doing it because it's your job, or because you want to get 'converts', or because some boss or superior will think better of you for your own benefit. One simply wants to serve.

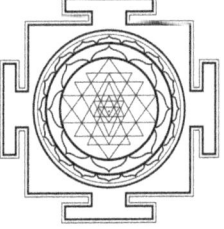

- Special morning on the lake -

- Shyamananda and a young deer -

7

1999:

Y2K Preparation

Some changes arrived on the shores of Inish Rath Island in 1999. Shyamananda Das, the temple president, decided to leave for Dublin to undertake a course in contemporary dance. He had been like a big brother for me, and I felt his loss. Part of his temple service was cooking a feast for the altar every day as part of some Vedic rituals going back millennia. As soon as he finished in the kitchen after several hours, he would rush off doing some project to help maintain the property in some way, like a working monk powerhouse. I wrote this poem the day he left.

An Engraved Plaque in Words

Stalking the corridors unseen
During the early hours
Simply leaving a scent
And presence in the showers

Flitting down the hallway
Pausing outside Bhagavat class
Breathing at keyhole catching the gist
Then sweeping out into the mist

And later back to cook for Krishna
Rock opera Song Divine ghettoblasts
Overhearers imagine effusive limbs
Dancing and twirling rolling pins!

…But, long drawn face deeply stretched
Minds surrender strained to test
Does service stifle freedom's space
Whilst something bright gushes muzzled?

The morning he left passed without incident
No bouquet, engraved plaque, or going away party
No "Congrats on X years service best wishes"
Just haribol in Ballyconnell

But as he was leaving I imagined
As Govindam prayers quickened to crescendo
At point where violin chorus enters
With two-waved high-set regal movement

And double bass resounds with power
Four descending notes vibrate the air
And gongs clash with imperial might
All instruments clarion call celestially

Here I imagined that – just this morning -
(Because spiritual things are sometimes ambiguous)
That the rousing fanfare played for Krishna
Was, just a touch, for His devotee too

Who'd given his heart in service
And from whom I've learned so much
But then he left and that night I turned to
Krishna and Balaram meet the inhabitants of Vrindavan

Because I was really thinking about the
Interactions and dealings of real people
As his discarded flipped slippers and departed spaces
Reminded me of the loss and all he had done.

Tulasi Priya Das became the new temple president. I have happy memories from this time, and I really enjoyed his daily lectures on the ancient text Srimad Bhagavatam. This 18,000-

verse text had been translated and commented upon by Srila Prabhupad who was the founder of the International Society for Krishna Consciousness. Prabhupad regarded this translation and commentary of the Bhagavatam as his most important literary service to humanity. Veda contains millions of words. However, Vyasadeva, or the literary incarnation of God, summarised the essence in the Bhagavatam (ref. Srimad Bhagavatam Canto 1, Chapter 5, plus Chapter 7 verses 1 to 10). This text is simultaneously mystical, and yet direct and accessible. Another name for this text is the *Bhagavat Purana*.

'This Bhagavat Purana is as brilliant as the sun, and it has arisen just after the departure of Lord Krishna to His own abode, accompanied by religion, knowledge, etc. Persons who have lost their vision due to the dense darkness of ignorance in this age of Kali shall get light from this Purana' (Srimad Bhagavatam 1.3.43).

Tulasi Priya Das had a thin, ageless face – a little birdlike in appearance – and he had practically no interest in consumerism, travel and frivolity. He was a man at home in a church or temple, and seemed a little out of place anywhere else. He had a philosophical outlook, and he was dependably always present. Meditation and temple life were his interests; not politics, management or money. If he had been an Englishman born in previous times, he would have been a vicar, or had he been born in India he would have been a temple Brahmin. Perhaps when his children were young, he wasn't *the* most fun-loving of fathers, but they will always be able to appreciate that he was stable, sane, dependable and never reckless.

Over the course of this year, I began working more with Manu Das. Manu had studied English at University College Dublin from 1979 until 1982, and then joined the temple the day after he finished the course. Although he had had a good relationship with his father and other family members, he had a strained relationship with his mother. His mother told him that if he didn't leave the Hare Krishna temple, she would cut him out of the property inheritance of the family home. By the time she passed away, he had never left Hare Krishna, and she kept her promise.

To raise income for the temple, many of the ashram residents in the '80s were sent out to sell oil paintings. As this was the only job he had ever known, he continued this into the 1990s, 2000s and the remainder of his working life. The name Manu in the Sanskrit language refers to the father of mankind. True to his name, he served the temple by being a provider, donating from the sales of artwork for decades, even when he was an independent family man with his own household expenses.

Manu's wife, Ishani, was a few years older than him, and she frequently verbally corrected him in public. One day I spoke privately to Manu. I was wondering how he could tolerate being told off so much. In my mind, I was wondering why he hadn't married a woman 10 years younger, a gentle and quiet partner. He instantly and ferociously stood up for his wife, correcting me. "Ishani has put up with so much from me over the years. She's a godsend, a serious devotee and a dedicated mother to our children." I stood corrected. I never mentioned anything like that to him again. I also appreciated the life lesson. Like an immature boy, I had been thinking a wife was meant to be a pretty girl who did what she was told, and didn't cause one too much hassle. I wasn't considering that a wife was a co-partner in the journey and adventure called life. Decades later, they are now a mature couple, and their adult children are living balanced and productive lives in stable marriages.

Manu had a slight tendency to be a dreamer, and Ishani often tried to bring him back to reality. For 25 years I listened to him as he came up with ideas to develop the temple. Several times he employed an architect to draw up elaborate plans for expansion. On paper, architects can draw up any fantasy fairytale temple; once one of them came up with a design for a purpose-built traditional structure with domes on the island. Manu was so disappointed when the price estimate came in as £10 million, when the island's entire annual income – year after year – was really only twice the size of the salary of an average Irish worker.

Manu bought a nine-seater minibus that allowed nine devotees of Krishna to go to Dublin every Saturday to chant the Hare Krishna mantra on the main shopping street. These were some of the happiest days of my life. The satisfaction that comes from sharing music, dance and mantra with shoppers, tourists and passers-by is – somehow or other – intense, deep and blissful. Multiplying the number of hours we were out by the average footfall on Grafton Street we must have shared the music with more than 20,000 people each Saturday.

Manu played the harmonium and he sang a particular tune which painted a picture of heaven through music, like a tone poem. He began slowly, meditatively, and gradually the tempo increased until everyone's hearts were dancing with joy. An enormous crowd formed on this pedestrian street and often four or eight people would spontaneously dance and laugh for the love of life. Some readers might be thinking, "The author here *might* be well meaning but he's a little simple; does he not know that people dance frivolously and jokingly with the Haris?" Yes, this is certainly the case at times, however, there are also times when an inexplicable Krishna magic descends from above, and everyone present experiences the tiniest droplet of pure love of God – something primal and long forgotten. The feeling is so beautiful that it gives one a momentary healthy doubt that our mission to find happiness forever through the medium of our own material mind and senses might just be a tad misplaced.

This kirtan or San-Kirtan is the gift of Shri Chaitanya, an avatar of Krishna. As Grafton Street's true and sometimes hidden spirituality was unfurling in the lotus of rhythm, our reverie would be broken by five Gardaí (Irish police) who would politely request we stop singing for five minutes so as to allow the crowd to disperse and move on. In our enthusiasm we hadn't noticed that the whole street had become clogged up with people like rush hour on the Tokyo subway. Anyway, our voice boxes appreciated the break. The physical and natural sound transmitters in our bodies' voice mechanisms were stretched trying to keep up with the esoteric enthusiasm.

***

Sports

Bhagavad Gita 6.17

He who is regulated in his habits of eating, sleeping, recreation and work can mitigate all material pains by practicing the yoga system.

In spite of the verse above where Krishna encourages people not to forget to be balanced in terms of eating, sleeping and relaxation, the International Society for Krishna Consciousness had been a religious movement where sports were looked down upon and people tended to spend a lot of time either preaching or struggling to keep temples open with limited income and resources.

In the summer of 1999, sponsored by Govinda's vegetarian restaurant in Dublin, we all had some uncharacteristic frivolity – we had a sports day. Football, chess, a 100m dash, a mini marathon, baseball, potato and spoon race, etc. it was the first time we were all relaxing with each other socially as humans rather than as being fellow missionaries, and it felt great.

It had been seven years since I had kicked a football and I was experiencing recreational ecstasy, messing around with the lads. I put together a ramshackle bunch to represent the island temple and we had a silly name *'The Inish Rath Warriors'*, a name that was all the more hilarious if you'd seen us in action. My only footwear was sandals and wellington boots, so I played barefoot wearing my Saffron robes. There is a way to tuck up a dhoti robe so one is less likely to trip over the flowing orange cotton.

Another event was the ultra mini-marathon which involved running three times around a looped road, taking about 20 minutes. My strap-on sandals could manage this, as there was no twisting, turning and kicking, like in football. Little did anyone else know but I had been in training for this for months, jogging around the circular perimeter track on the island.

As my body is shorter than average for an Irishman, in the sporting arena no one really expects me to be victorious. The race started and I began to pace myself, staying beside or behind several fellow racers. From the opening gunshot, tall and strong Randy Repass from California was out in front. Slowly, slowly I built up momentum, passing the other racers and coming comfortably into second place. We looped around for the final circuit and the finish line. The ribbon crossed the width of the road and this was in sight, flanked by crowds of cheering spectators. Building up a measured pace I accelerated into a sprint, passed by Randy, crossed the finish line, broke the ribbon, and won the gold medal. It was just a hoot, *slightly* resembling a pre-teen underdog movie where the little guy goes through some struggle but comes out on top in the end. All good fun and Randy sportingly and sincerely congratulated the boy holding the top spot on the podium.

Speaking of Randy Repass Jr., another time I heard that Randy Repass Senior from the USA was coming to visit his son on Inish Rath Island.

Mr. Repass was a millionaire who had a successful business. Someone told me he'd just arrived on a boat, and I looked out the window expectantly. In my mind, I was excited. I'd never seen a millionaire before. I think I was expecting someone extravagant, like a gold medallion draped around his neck *or* several assistants buzzing around, waiting for his next command. In the distance, I got a glimpse of the man, and as he approached he came more into view. And then I could see him. He was wearing jeans, a tee-shirt and a baseball cap. I was flummoxed. *He* is a millionaire?! He looked like a typical American tourist that one might see anywhere in the world. This temple boy was almost disappointed.

Years later I had an interaction with him when he rented a room from me during a visit to our local area. I had an impression that he was sensible, pleasant and friendly.

***

On August 22nd 1999, a full colour, full page broadsheet article appeared on the back of the weekend section of the Sunday Independent, the largest newspaper in the country at that time. This newspaper had a readership of one fifth of the population of the island of Ireland at the end of the century.

There were photos of Manu and his two small children, Jayananda and Sita, and another photo of a young, saffron robed monk studying a 2,000-page translation of an ancient Sanskrit text. This was me. The article was about our Inish Rath Island Visitor Centre and the opening of our reclusive ashram for the general public. I had sent a simple typed letter to the editor's desk and somehow our little story piqued some interest. It was exciting to be involved in positive news which was read – or at least seen – by several hundred thousand people.

***

We had signs down by the lake inviting passing boat-tourists to come up and visit the temple. I was regularly showing little groups of up to eight people into the shrine area. I always included a few words about the culture and teachings, and answered any of the questions of these visitors. In Ireland, there are only really a handful of hot days per year, and most of the time, including the summer, the temperature is fresh. In the modern day, our country has no dress regulations for visiting churches. Our climate ensures that people generally wear more clothing as a requirement for keeping warm and dry. However, one memorable summer day, two rare events occurred. Number one: it was scorching hot. And number two: this terrified young monk was faced with providing a tour to two very beautiful and very scantily clad French girls.

Our Visitor Centre had signs welcoming tourists, and the building, outwardly, just looks like a sizeable old country house, rather than a place of worship. So, I wasn't prepared for this one. The two girls in their early twenties came off a boat, looking to take a tour of the temple. Hundreds of millions of men around the world will agree that a quietly confident, attractive French woman is the epitome of enchanting femininity. *Les Mademoiselles* were wearing bikini tops, earrings, jewellery… they were dressed to be noticed. I had been facing in the opposite direction, and then I turned around, and there they were: ready for a tour, as promised by our signage. I gulped. With an innocent glance, one of the girls asked me if they could come on the tour. She had the most seductive accent imaginable. There was no one else around. This was new.

"Do I tell them they have to dress more modestly in the temple?" I thought.

But I was actually just trying to keep myself together and not stutter. My mind raced. We had no signage instructing people on a dress code, and what they were wearing is legal for this country, so what was I going to say? Besides, if I even began to refer to their clothing, I might get myself into some trouble. These goddesses had a cryptic and alluring power, and I was doing my best to look detached. I reasoned that the best thing was to just do a short tour and get it over with. So that is what I did. After the tour ended, the girls returned to their hired cruiser boat. As they glided away, they both turned around to wave and smile. Standing there in the saffron robes of a monk, I waved back. Outwardly I attempted to look completely detached from the external world, but in truth I was slightly overwhelmed.

***

Christmas Day, 1999. Around 30 of us gathered in the temple's conference room to watch a film about Jesus. I understand it was the one and only time in the history of the temple there was a group cinema experience. We had a TV / video player for the guided tours that usually showed tourists a short video about the culture, so this was used. By this stage, I hadn't watched TV for six years and six months, so I sat, eyes glued to the screen, enjoying every second of this visual pleasure. I lapped up the movie like a thirsty man in a desert finds water. Imagine the inner joy of a man lost for days in the Canadian wilderness. He eventually finds a friendly village and is offered an armchair by a roaring fire, a hot drink and sweet words by villagers. I was sparkling and exuberant up to this level of pleasure, lounging back and drinking in the Jesus movie through my eyes and ears!

***

Spread by conspiracy theorists, or by businessmen selling programmes designed to counteract the alleged problem, a rumour was being widely circulated that computers were going to reset to 0000000 on January the 1st 2000.

As civilisation had become more and more dependent on and linked up to computers, the rumour was that systems around the world would blank out a millisecond after midnight – so electricity, water, telephone, military, banking, petroleum, law, justice, police, retail and transport – all these systems and services would collapse and everyone would have to fend for themselves in a post-apocalyptic world where horses, bows & arrows, potatoes and blackberry fruits took on new importance.

As Hare Krishna people already had a tendency to be slightly anti-mainstream, quite a few of the devotees were either going along with it, or were at least preparing for the worst. Some of the bigger men were actually buying bows and arrows, just in case.

Shyamananda Das (now living in Dublin, but sometimes visiting us at Inish Rath) had just received a small inheritance of several thousand Irish pounds from an old uncle (a Catholic priest) who had died, so he purchased many sacks of oats, rice, beans, salt and so on, just in case.

On New Year's Eve, as the Millennium came to a hesitant close, the island's temple room was packed full of devotees chanting and singing. On the stroke of midnight someone standing in the adjacent hallway snuck their hand through a little gap in the door and turned off all the lights, flicking the switches with mischievous intent. In that still and calm moment where heartbeats could be heard, everyone was thinking the same thing, "Oh my God this is it: civilisation as we know it is gone."

"No electricity"

"Simple weapons"

"Drinking water with cupped hands from the lake"

"I'll never see blackberry brambles as weeds again"

"Teaching kids about wild herbs in hedge schools"

"How does one make a spray to control potato blight?"

These thoughts, and more, passed through many minds simultaneously.

The lights were flicked back on after 10 seconds, and I wouldn't be surprised if there were not a handful of people who were slightly disappointed that civilisation was still trundling along as normal. Electricity, machines, computers and petroleum usage got to live another glorious noisy day. But one cannot but be slightly amazed by the ruthless entrepreneurship of the Y2K merchandisers who, if nothing else, are certainly expert salespeople.

I had personally missed this action, but heard about it later from Aniruddha (Andy). I had decided to share chant and music with people on Grafton Street in Dublin for the turn of the millennium. I teamed up with a young man from an English temple who was visiting the country and the two of us set up on the pedestrian street and sang, and laid out Krishna books for passers-by to see. My parents kindly welcomed my English friend and myself to stay in their house overnight. Being almost penniless, I did have to do something to make money for bus fares, so a few days earlier in the temple I had unearthed an old Hare Krishna festival poster under piles of stuff in a disused room. The image on the poster was the most attractive image of child Krishna imaginable. I had found a frame, used a paper blade, did some picture tidying up, and then it appeared as a framed painting. On the street this was laid out with the books, and I wrote 'For Sale'. I remember one businessman briskly walking by, when from the corner of his eye he saw Krishna. He stopped abruptly, backtracked, and stood looking at Krishna with fascination. "How much is this?" he said. "£20," said I, and he whipped out the purple note. He chirpily walked off with Krishna tucked under his arm.

- Painting of Krishna as a boy -

- Janaki and beads -

8

2000:

Learning to Love Together

As the bright new Millennium began, I started travelling out with Manu Das for three days and two nights per week, beginning with an early morning departure every Tuesday. In preparation, to help my focus for the austerity, I did a full fast from food on Monday. We drove for three or four hours and then I would stand on the streets of large towns to distribute Krishna conscious books while Manu sold art: mostly paintings of landscapes, nature and European period buildings. His business collected money for his family expenses, but also he was the main donor for the temple.

Manu had spent decades juggling money in order to keep the temple running. I remember one day we were driving between Limerick and Galway while there were major road-works, probably motorway construction. Manu had some money which needed to be lodged into the temple's bank account before bills reduced the balance to below zero, with no overdraft facility available. We came over a hump in the road and ahead of us was a long, worrying line of cars stalled at temporary traffic lights. With the clock ticking away before the bank in the next town was going to close, Manu began accelerating rather than slowing down. I side glanced apprehensively, muscles tightened, mentally preparing for the brace position. Suddenly, like a scene from an action movie, we were speeding down the hard shoulder to *the side of the traffic jam*, fast and furious, accelerating – caution thrown to the wind.

As the temporary lights turned red Manu swerved to the side, tyres screeching and cut in just ahead of another car, sped on towards the town, came to an abrupt halt in front of the bank, leapt out, flew up the steps and slapped down a wad of cash in front of the cashier. Never a dull moment in the service of Krishna! Another day with the temple bills getting paid, just about.

***

On this trip away from the temple I ended up catching flu. It was the first time I had had flu in eight or nine years. Apart from in India when I had stomach and digestion issues, the only other time I was sick was the occasional blocked nose or sore throat. So, I went to convalesce in the house of a Hare Krishna couple. He was originally German, and she was from Galway. It was the best place in the world to suffer health challenges. They treated me like royalty. I got to watch television, which was a huge treat, as I hadn't seen flickering images on a screen since early 1993. On VHS video tapes I watched spiritual and Krishna conscious videos. Of course, I wasn't going to watch standard channels like RTE and BBC. The cheerful couple kept checking to see if I was okay, and they brought me fresh juice and herbal tea several times a day. As I began to improve after a few days they cooked delicious but healthy meals for me. It was the most enjoyable flu I've ever had! I think it was Krishna's arrangement to give me a relaxation holiday, and to get their wonderful association. Four years before this they had been living in Germany, but thinking of moving to Ireland. I had exchanged letters with them about coming over to the island temple, and they had stayed on the island for several weeks.

***

Later on that year the Inish Rath temple was blessed by the visit of a special personality. His Holiness Bhakti Tirtha Swami had come from an African American Christian background, and he exuded gentleness, enthusiasm and love. In 1976 he shared Krishna consciousness in Eastern Europe where preaching was often illegal and many people he came into contact with had never actually seen a black person. Often, he marched into the philosophy, theology or psychology department of some university and managed to sell books about Vedic wisdom. He didn't speak the local language and, according to the governments of those times, it was illegal to promote religion. Once, in the former East Germany, a university professor pretended to be interested, and then directed the swami to a certain building to 'another professor'. Bhakti Tirtha and his German-speaking assistant made their way to this other place, religious books in hand, only to find they had been tricked into being sent to the police. As the other devotee began to contemplate how long they would have to spend in a dingy prison, BT Swami proceeded to give beaming smiles, told jokes, displayed loving friendly behaviour, and basically with sweet words – translated into German – he stated that he wasn't really aware of the local law. Fortunately, the authorities ended up releasing them. They left that place, and simply went onto another university and just carried on with their mission to share spiritual life.

Selling books isn't simply a commercial enterprise designed to make money — there are far easier ways to earn a living. Rather, unless a book-buyer is convinced enough of the potential usefulness of the literature they won't release hard-earned money. If they get something for free, they often may not take it seriously, but the act of paying for the literature increases the chance that the book will be respected and read. On top of that, the book printing must be paid for.

✱✱✱

Mangala Arati is the first ceremony and chant of the day. It's inspiring to start the day from 4.30am with these chants and prayers. However, our own minds are there niggling away distracting us, always looking for a new thing, a next experience. It's often because we are not mindful enough that we can't see the beauty in what is already there, so, at times, as the weeks change into months and these months build up to year after year, one's mind is saying, "Here we are, the same place, same people, same music year after year. I feel trapped. Can we not do something different?" So as a small handful of Irish people were struggling away to keep the morning programme going daily, one day a shining black man danced into the temple room with a white and wholesome beaming smile. He began playing a huge African drum (which looked like an oversized bodhrán) and lovingly directed everyone to dance from one end of the temple room to the other. Our usual sleepy morning was transformed into the ecstasy of kirtan as this monk, who had also been honoured as a High Chief in an African country (in 1990), exuded love and warmth. When the tempo builds up in a kirtan to this day I can still feel the effects of what BT Swami was freely giving out that morning.

In the summer of 2000, our green and wooded island ashram also welcomed a German swami and Tribhuvanatha Das, plus a youth group of British Indians called the *Pandava Sena*. Tribhuvanatha had stationed me on the island five years before and it was wonderful to see him again. The German swami, a saffron-robed monk, sounded shockingly gentle and jolly. From English WW2-set comic books in 1982 my seven-year-old self thought 'Germans' were bad guys, such that I cried when Germany beat France in the soccer World Cup final. But those comic book writers maybe needed to meet more Germans like this man. He was genuinely light and funny while at the same time he was able to communicate wisdom in an innocent way. And, oh the eighties! I'm not sure what a seven-year-old was doing reading WW2 battle comic books with grenades, tanks and soldiers getting killed. Hmmm.

The two senior devotees gave talks to the enthusiastic youth. Placing 50 boys and girls aged 16 to 24 together on an island for a five-day retreat creates a real buzz. Not only is there natural spiritual enthusiasm, but some of the youths are also wondering who could be their future spouses. Impassioned chemistry, flashing smiles and yearnings for happiness on many levels are all jumbled up in an uncorrupted immature fusion, so the whole event has a wonderful energy. When all the action was over after several days, everyone was very emotional departing. In the minds of the guests, they had come for a break from London, and had found a little heaven. Heaven was created by people coming together and acting as they should – loving relationships guided by elders all praying and learning together.

After several days they were returning to their usual daily challenges. I was slowly pacing up and down outside Inish Rath House murmuring mantras on wooden beads. As everyone was leaving, a young woman could hardly contain her emotion, and suddenly she jumped off the boat and ran the quarter of a kilometre back to the golden shrine of the temple. A few friends ran after her, perhaps to help convince her it was now time to go 'back to reality' - life, education, work, commuting, earning, family, etc. A 'Vaishnava' is someone in the religious family of Krishna, Vishnu or Rama, which are various names of God within the Vedic worldview. A 'Vaishnavi' is a specifically feminine use of the word, with the final syllable rhyming with *glee*. That evening I wrote a poem about the whole event.

Learning to Love Together

Embracing the men, or wanting to
And asking names again
They're going, and wanting to savour time
And say *thank you*
Assemblage of Vaishnavas
Youth, beauty, hope
And shimmering waters
Govinda stages shining sun
Freezing gem-like moment.

Really seeing how great Vaishnavas really are,
Ours and theirs, now it's clear
Exalted souls standing there, me teeth-clench shy
Heavy tears and loving embraces,
Then wrenching free, striking up the path
Force and glee a Vaishnavi aims for Govinda's feet
Like a released arrow of depth
Three arrows zip after in hot pursuit
Striking gold and chanting in rapture –
With feeling – as I mumble outside fingering beads
Tasting time for the future.

Chanting in San-kirtan means we're in this together
We're learning to love together
I close off but I hope I can release,
And turn and face and dance in harmony.

***

Around this time there was a little gossip going around the corridors of Inish Rath House. Mo (Mahotsaha Das / Mark Prunty) - originally from England and serving in the temples in Ireland since December 1993 - fell in love with Nitai, a girl who had lived several years of her childhood at the island temple. There was a slight scandal, as he was 29 and she was only 16. Some older members of the community were grumbling and spreading rumours of inappropriate behaviour.

Nitai's mother, a single mother, had raised Nitai and her younger sister either in or living close to the temple. This lovely and sincere lady seemed occasionally troubled. I think she seemed to veer between wishing she herself was in a normal happy marriage to - more often - wishing she could renounce her responsibilities and surrender to the Lord as a full-time monastic. Nitai later described herself as the love-child of a Hare Krishna nun and a pirate, her absent father. In the end, everything worked out. Mo is now 53 and Nitai is 40, and they have four wonderful children. Nitai's mother made it through raising her two girls by herself, and she's now delighted to be a grandmother, plus she's free to do as much monastic activity as she likes.

- Temple room -

- Tribhuvanatha Das -

9

2001:

Dublin

In the '70s and '80s the year 2001 was depicted with futuristic skyscrapers, lasers, robots, and perhaps family holidays on Mars for richer folk. When we got there the only thing that had really made it were the skyscrapers – but not in Ireland. Manu Das told me once that on a business trip to New York he stayed in a skyscraper hotel and he couldn't sleep properly all night - imagining the swaying, and having trust-issues with the work of the engineers. I'd probably do the same myself.

As the world adjusted to being fairly and squarely in a new Millennium, Manu began to doubt he could carry on being the main fund-raiser for the temple. For just an ordinary man with a slightly above-average income, it was a lot to ask. And it wasn't like he had a comfortable job, and was collecting a salary from the donations. No – he himself was often the main donor.

The other handful of residents who lived on the mainland across from the island at that time were just about able to pay their own bills, having given their youth to sharing Krishna consciousness and preaching. So a decision was made to put the island property on the market with a general plan to use the proceeds of the sale to buy a property in the Dublin region.

Meanwhile I turned 26 in March and I had a minor personal crisis. "Oh God," I thought, "I'm getting older." Apart from the £20 inserted into birthday cards by my mother and Aunt Frances, I was penniless. The Mammy and Aunty money had been paying for my socks and toothpaste for years. Trousers – although I mostly wore robes – jerseys, coats and footwear tended to be what visitors accidentally left behind, or just what someone gave me. Not being tall, I was often left with baggy jumpers and enormous coats. Being excited to explore the joys of romance one day I knew that meant being out in the world and making money, so I developed a plan to return to university and carry on studying general science. My one-year break in 1993 had turned into an eight year sabbatical.

I applied to UCD and was accepted. One day, I got chatting to a Spanish woman who was visiting the island temple. She was returning to her home country for six weeks and was looking for a house-sitter. So, I found myself back in my own home city of Dublin with somewhere to stay for free. However, there was a catch.

I was supposed to mind my host's dog, but after only one night I remembered I wasn't really a dog person at all. Fortunately for me I'd recently done a favour for one man. One of his businesses was dog minding, so the next day the dog was taken away to a better place. What a relief… I don't know what I was thinking agreeing to that.

The apartment was home to a wide variety of scattered random items which were strewn over the floor and table-tops, plus dog hairs, grime and clutter. It became my mission to transform the space. When she returned from Spain six weeks later the woman got the shock of her life to walk into a silent, Zen meditation space – uncluttered and minimalistic. I had already left by that stage, and the dog minder kindly returned her four-legged friend. I think I may have been guilty of throwing out some stuff which I judged to be rubbish, but the woman may have wanted.

During my few weeks staying there I wrote this poem:

'One morning in Ballymun'

> The morning sun alights dreary Ballymun
> Shines on the rusty shabby degenerate things
> Broken glass and concrete pillars
> Frustrated slogans and plastic wrappers pause
> Heartless erections from an urban calculator
> All stand before a new day of God
> Who overpowers the general despair
> And magics the glass on the pavement
> To look like scattered diamonds
> Sparkling with the majesty of Creation.

***

I was back in the city. Praghosa Das offered me a job doing book-keeping for Govinda's vegetarian restaurant, an informal Krishna-themed eatery selling good value, hot meals. I went to stay with my dear elderly Aunt Frances in my mother's family home 45 minutes' walk from the city centre. Tuberculosis during her youth had resulted in long hospitalisation and poor health, and with very little appetite she weighed only 30 to 35kg. Frances was religious, meek and dependably always present at home. She never married but she liked to mother my brother, sister and me in a very quiet, gentle and unassuming way.

We were always welcome in her home. In my life I feel blessed to have had her association.

***

When I returned to Dublin, I was still a monk wearing saffron robes when we went out every Saturday afternoon to sing and chant in the city centre. A man who wants to wear Indian clothes as a Hare Krishna man, but who isn't a monk, is not allowed to wear saffron orange robes; the standard colour is white, or sometimes the kurta (shirt) top can be other colours also, but saffron is only for monks. A shy and pretty 20-year-old daughter of Hare Krishna parents had come to Dublin from Venezuela, and she was taking part in the Harinam public chanting sessions with us. The girl had come to study. I asked the temple authority, Manu, to ask her if she'd like to investigate marrying me. He said that Medhavi Nimai Das (Mick Duff) had already asked him the same question. She politely responded through Manu that she had only come to study English for a few months in Dublin, and then she was returning home, and she had a life elsewhere. But, anyway, just before Manu popped the question, I figured out that I can hardly be a monk anymore while asking questions like this, so it was time to stop wearing the saffron robes. I gave them away to men who were still monks. In Asian religious culture, there are student monks. It's expected that almost all of them will marry in the future. However, while they are monks they are supposed to put aside plan-making and simply train in meditation and culture. So, one tries to put aside making plans, but we don't always do things perfectly, do we?

In the late summer of 2001, I visited Inish Rath Island when senior monk and dynamic preacher of Krishna Consciousness Tribhuvanatha Das was also staying for a few days. He appeared simultaneously jolly, while also being grave and deep. Within the last year he had developed cancer and it was believed to be very serious. In the temple room he blessed me saying, "Timmy, you're always here," referring to me being stationed on the island temple. I didn't want to let him know that I had left the island, and was really only visiting. His daughter came to see him. She was 19. I didn't even know he had a daughter. During the early '80s he had been briefly married in England, but a few years later he couldn't contain the call to become a spiritual preacher and sharer of wisdom. I don't know any details of his short married life.

With Tribhuvanatha walking around and radiating a sublime sense of peace I somehow assumed he would recover physically. He didn't. He departed from the world on October 16th 2001. The International Governing Body of the Society decreed that the local annual religious calendar for Great Britain and Ireland should honour him with a mention on the date of his departure from this world. That was the only time they've done this. Bhaktivedanta Manor, the main temple of our home islands, purchased a car for his daughter, as Tribhuvanatha had wanted to get her one. However, as he used all the donations he got in sharing love with others, he had no significant personal money. I always remembered that kind deed. It surprised me, pleasantly. Our temple upbringing had been 'Everything is for the Mission' so hearing a temple buying a blood relative a material product seemed so down-to-earth to me. It seemed so human, in contrast to the usual other-worldly stance.

***

Return to University

It's thrilling to arrive at a university in the morning time: young people everywhere, full of hope, their lives ahead of them, learning, trying to figure out how to make civilisation greater. Within the first few days I was called into a small room for some personal guidance on how things were operating now. Coincidentally, the man showing me the ropes had been in my year in '93 and he remembered the shy boy who got up in front of the physics lecture hall and appealed for donations for charity.

In my first session, the instructor said, "Blah, blah, blah, something, something... and then copy and paste that... etc." I looked blankly.

"Something something **copy** and **paste**," he stressed the last two words.

I imagined in half a second writing out some words on paper, cutting out the section with scissors, and gluing down this paper somewhere. My continued confused expression had the young lecturer explaining what *copy and paste* on a computer meant.

"Have you been on a desert island, or something?" he laughed.

"Not exactly a ***desert*** island," I whispered.

At the university, the science buildings were grouped around each other in a formation: physics on one wing, chemistry on another, and then biology. All three were connected with glass corridors to a central science lecture space. Once I overheard faculty members in one wing criticising their colleagues in another branch of science.

"Ahh ha, they do this here too," I thought.

I had lived in a religious community for so many years that I forgot the same kinds of things go on everywhere. We have a tendency to subtly try to put others down, so as to try to appear greater or more wonderful ourselves. And the funny thing is it doesn't even work. We lose our honour when we criticise. That is not to say that we can't denounce poor behaviour in others; but when our inward motivation is self-glorification in an egotistical fashion, then we end up fooling ourselves. We might be in a religious community doing this, or we might be in a village, a city workplace, a hairdressers, or on a ship 400 miles out at sea. Fault-finding seems to be a recurring practise of the human condition.

***

At the end of the year for some inspiration to see a larger and well-organised temple in operation, I popped over on a bus to England to visit Bhaktivedanta Manor, in the countryside adjacent to London. Sivarama Swami was hosting a Christmas Marathon event to appreciate all the devotees who went out in December to distribute books on the cold streets of towns and cities in the United Kingdom.

The leading distributors in the UK were called up to receive a small gift of gratitude, and who did I see among them, but Monk Peter from Lisburn, Northern Ireland! This is the man whose Brahmin underwear had gone up in flames in 1994, and who accompanied me to India in 1996. Now, like myself, Peter (now Premarnava Das) was a little shy, but this monk was also kind, gentle and extremely polite. Commonly, the top Krishna book sellers were enthusiastic and outgoing people, who could address crowds, give speeches and are comfortable as the centre of attention at an event.

It was curious and satisfying to see such an unassuming man in the limelight as a book distributing leader. It was like he came through, in the end. Back in the mid-1990s, he had always distributed the least amount of books. Some days he couldn't hack it on the street, and he'd give up and just go to a health food shop and find tasty eatables to gorge over. But, now, all the other boys were no longer wearing the saffron robes of a monk, but Monk Peter was still doing his best to share spiritual wisdom with humanity.

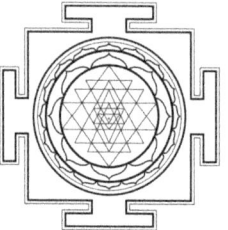

- Kirtan chanting on the streets of Dublin -

- Kirtan in Dublin temple -

10

2002:

UCD

I carried on with the science degree course at University College Dublin while starting to miss the tranquillity of Inish Rath Island. I would cycle around Dublin looking for a place of remote stillness in nature, but faced a slight challenge in finding what I was looking for.

I was undertaking the course with a vague plan to use the degree to help in getting some job, but I had another motivation, which I will now explain. Although a majority of people in the world are nominally connected to some religion, in practice secular science demands a huge amount of faith.

If one looks at 99% of educational institutions in the world, they're teaching a worldview through the lens of modern, secular science. This way of seeing the world is so widespread that many people would think it laughable to consider believing anything else.

Some major worldviews *loosely* categorised are:

(1) Secular science - Agnostic or Atheist;

(2) Judeo-Christian / Islamic views with God, prophets, heaven and hell;

(3) Vedic (Hinduism) with God, demigods, karma and reincarnation;

(4) Nature-based systems with spirits and reincarnation - witches, shamans, etc; and

(5) Buddhism - spiritual agnostics.

In our modern world with many operating machines, systems and the internet, the worldviews of the majority of people would be a strong dose of secular science mixed up with whatever other religion or path we feel attracted to, or are born into.

These categorisations are fluid and general: a majority of people would not neatly fit into only one viewpoint, but are quite accepting of concepts from several categories. Some Jews, Christians and Muslims would not appreciate being categorised in the same general group, but here we're just taking a theological glance at what university scholars refer to as Abrahamic religion.

Hare Krishna people, the actual name for their religion being Gaudiya Vaishnavism, see the world from the Vedic point of view. Atheists with strong faith in material science would be facing across from the Krishna devotee on the debating table.

In one belief, no one created the universe - it just happened. Inert matter got itself together to create complex form, and now that we humans have desires and our own measurable form, our goal is to be as happy as we can be within our bodies. When we die, it's all over. Our essence was matter, and that matter has simply merged with other matter.

The Vedic point of view is that Krishna, through Vishnu *avatars* (expansions) created the Universe to fulfil the desires of souls who wanted a break from loving Krishna. Krishna - He mentions in passing – doesn't *need* our love; however things are just better when we all love each other, and Krishna. We do that in the spiritual world, but due to independence we can leave there if we want to. So at some point we desired a break from the spiritual world, and therefore we came down to the world of matter. The material world has wonderful aspects like tropical lagoons, sunrises, rainbows, nice people and hugs; however, if one looks closely, the material world also has violence, disease and decay everywhere.

In the Bhagavad Gita and Srimad Bhagavatam – primary Vedic texts – Krishna suggests to us that we are better off re-establishing our relationship with Him, and this will result in us returning home to our original form. However, He then leaves it up to us to make the choice as to what we want to do (see BG 18.63).

The teachings suggest that when we arrived in the material world for the first time (Veda indicates this could have been billions of years ago) we initially had an elevated heavenly body. However, due to contact with other souls who had taken on a material form, karma began. This led to reincarnation, which led to revolving around the wheel of *Samsara* again and again.

Veda suggests our goal should be to meditate and aspire to offer pure devotional service through developing bhakti, or pure love. At the highest stage of bhakti, it doesn't really matter whether we are in the material world or the spiritual world because wherever we are, we will be with Krishna.

To return to the earlier point, an atheist scientist and a theistic Gaudiya Vaishnava may stand as opponents in a formal, philosophical debate. I had an idea that studying science (the 'opposition') would be useful in debates and in sharing Krishna consciousness. Scientists don't have to be in opposition to theistic theology, but currently most of them choose to be so.

I had such an inspirational time being a student monk from 1993 until 2001 that I naturally felt inclined to share the joy with others. During a visit to Dublin by His Holiness Bhakti Vikasa Swami, known for his conservative and 'old-school' views, I rented a hotel conference room for one of his lectures. About 50 people came along. This swami has strong opinions about certain traditional topics, or at least that's how many contemporary people see things. One evening, my sister Barbara (then 20) attended one of his lectures and introduced me to her boyfriend John-Michael (24). Coming from the Irish countryside and a Mass-goer, John-Michael appreciated the lecture, but my dear sister – not so much! Since that time this swami has written a book called Mothers and Masters. His first printing of this book was banned by the Hare Krishna Society internationally as being likely to cause offence to certain Western sensibilities on women's issues. He made adjustments to subsequent printings of the book to allow it to be available for sale in Krishna temples, although some temple councils still don't connect with it.

Later, when I was introduced to John-Michael he was speaking in a slurred voice, and I was very concerned he was intoxicated. "Is he okay, Barbara?" I said quietly in a tone that was *really* asking,

"Is *he* the one for you? He seems drunk to me."

Years later I found out that he had just come from a rugby match and had a concussion that caused the slurred speech. He had come along anyway to get to know our family, and he is now her husband and is very much right for her.

In the spring of 2002, I spotted the Taoiseach (head of the Government of Ireland), Bertie Ahern, who was out on the campaign trail and talking with citizens. I approached him and saw his security people glancing at me, but they didn't stop me. We got talking about Hare Krishna and he commented that he used to see them chanting on the streets in the 1980s, but not so much anymore. I told him it's a bit like that all over the world, at least in Western countries. We shook hands warmly. He struck me as someone who shook an awful lot of hands.

***

Next, I had the opportunity to serve others by restarting a Sunday programme for the general public. In Krishna temples around the world the Sunday Feast offers a delicious free meal, music, chanting and a lecture. Devotees who cooked all week for Govinda's Restaurant had to cook again for the Sunday Feast, which left a big mess for them to clean up on their day off. As a result they were exhausted. So I had a plan to skip the free meal and just do the lecture and mantra music. We had a regular attendance of about twenty to twenty five people who enjoyed partaking in the musical offering and listening to the lecture. Anuragi gave the talk a few times. She was only aged about 21 or 22 at the time, and everyone else in the room was older than her, but she saw it as a service to talk about spiritual life, bhakti and Krishna. Although she was not an outgoing person, everyone was impressed with her quiet, humility-driven confidence and sincerity. A team of four Hungarian girls in their early to mid-twenties were in Dublin to distribute books about Krishna. In Gaudiya Vaishnava (Hare Krishna) theology it is fairly widely understood that it is quite possible that a girl of 18 or 20 years old can be more spiritually advanced than a man who is 20 or even 50 years older. Spiritual maturity can be built up over multiple lifetimes.

***

In 2002, I cycled daily to and from the university, crossing the city centre from Cabra in the Northwest, to UCD on the Southside. One day, as I was cycling along a major road a young man driving from a minor road approached the junction without stopping. He hadn't noticed that I was there, didn't stop, and I ended up getting launched into the air and rolling on, and subsequently off, the bonnet of his car. It was clearly the driver's fault. My legs, knees and hands were bloody and shaking. The young man briefly came towards me, checked that I wasn't dead, and then quickly drove off. A crowd of passers-by began to form and people were inquiring about my welfare. Someone helped me to retrieve my mangled bicycle. A moment later, a concerned Garda approached me. He had seen the accident from a distance.

"Are you okay?" he said.

"I have the registration number of that car… would you like to press charges?" the Garda continued.

And then I replied, with my knees dripping blood and my bike warped:

"…Ahh, sure, I'll be fine…"

And that was that.

My one and only chance to sue someone for damages disappeared as quickly as it had arisen. I hobbled away in pain, and recovered a week later.

Why did I not press charges? I figured it was my karma to experience that pain, and as it wasn't major, I didn't want to bother the legal system, as they had more important matters to deal with.

***

Arranged Marriage

For Westerners, lovers of individual liberty, the very sight of the two words 'arranged' and 'marriage' together can bring to mind stories like in the following examples. A 17-year-old girl born in Europe to Asian parents is flown across the world on the pretence of meeting, and perhaps one day marrying, a handsome young doctor. To her horror she finds herself trapped and abused by a beast 10 years older than her father.

Or, somewhere in Asia, a 14-year-old is bundled into a car at night by two older brothers and driven along dusty roads for seven hours. The next morning an envelope exchanges hands, the brothers depart, and the unfortunate girl is sold into slavery, where she is verbally, emotionally and physically exploited by her new family. She's forced to marry the 30-year-old son.

There is actually quite a difference between a forced marriage, condemned by decent folk everywhere, and an arranged marriage. In fact, most marriages in India to this day are arranged marriages, and the practise has been going on for millennia. There are many examples of respectable families matching up a young couple to the satisfaction of all. My experience of this practise is almost non-existent, but I wanted to briefly give an example of where *some* arrangement has the potential to make the world a better place.

I was wondering who to get married to, so I found a new Hare Krishna marriage website on the internet. I began an email conversation with a devotee who was probably in his early '50s at that time. He and his family lived in North Carolina, USA. He had lived in the temple in the 1970s, but was now a working family man. His daughter was 18. He was checking me out, and asking many questions, and then consulting with his daughter. I actually never got to communicate with her personally. After he was somewhat satisfied that I didn't appear to be lazy or crazy, the next stage was an astrological compatibility check.

After some weeks, the astrologer responded and it appeared we were not compatible according to the stars and the universe. The father later told me that they had decided to investigate things further with a young man in Poland who spoke good English.

The next stage, apparently, was that the girl and the boy would communicate through writing themselves, and then, later, there may be a face-to-face meeting, all with the father carefully protecting his daughter, but at the same time allowing freedom to choose.

Assuming that this father in North Carolina was being truthful with me (I had no reason to suspect otherwise), all-in-all, the entire procedure seemed quite sensible, for those who wish to use methods like this.

- Inish Rath Island – aerial view -

- A Forest walk on Inish Rath -

11

2003:

Four Hungarian Girls

In the early part of the year I began going out alone to Grafton Street, Dublin, to chant with the harmonium. I owned a traditional keyboard harmonium that sounded like a miniature church organ. I also carried out a microphone and stand, and books for passers-by. I sang slowly and calmly into the microphone for several hours. I had asked an artist who was visiting the country from Australia to make a mantra board with the Hare Krishna Mantra written in an attractive font, and embellished with flower and leaf designs around it, so I brought this as well. The whole set-up was too heavy to carry, so I had a trolley. As I was singing, a busker came up to me and said grumpily, "Hey fella, that's *my* spot." He started to fume and rant that I had taken his busking spot. I paused, looked at him, and prayed to work out what was the best thing to do in this situation. A small crowd of seven or eight random people formed instantly and almost mysteriously, and they all chipped in and told this man that this wasn't his spot at all. It was a free country and a free street and anyone could come here and sing. They banded together and told him he should go on his way. He muttered, fumbled, cursed and argued, but he couldn't fight against a crowd, so frustrated, he took his stuff and carried on. I never saw him again. I had never even opened my mouth. I smiled and nodded at the passers-by, they smiled at me, and the chanting continued.

On Saturdays, tens of thousands of people pass by the top of Grafton Street across the road from the beautiful tended gardens of Saint Stephen's Green. This is a favourite location for buskers and street performers. I decided to ask for special permission from the Gardaí (police force) to occupy that spot on March the 1st 2003, so in early January I found myself in the Garda superintendent's office explaining what I wanted to do. 'Prayer for peace: Chanting 100,000 names of God.'

I explained to him that we planned to sing all day in an effort to promote peace, harmony and universal brotherhood. Lust to enjoy something that isn't ours, greed, jealousy, uncontrolled anger, frustration, laziness and hate are all lower qualities that are fundamental causes of war and unrest. Chanting holy mantras with music purifies the heart. When this kirtan is taken out to a public place it becomes san-kirtan, the complete kirtan. The vast wisdom of the Veda, expressed through millions of Sanskrit words, is summarised in the 18,000-verse Srimad Bhagavatam. The final verse of the Bhagavatam specifically encourages Sankirtan as the next thing to do on putting down the book.

With a little help from a calculator, I worked out that if I started the recitation of mantras myself on wooden prayer beads at 4.00am, the others could join me in singing between 10.00am and noon time. By evening I estimated we would have recited 100,000 holy names. Police Superintendent John Keenan was accommodating and helpful. Just before I turned to leave, he remarked that he would send some of the boys by during the early hours to ensure I was okay. I smiled politely in gratitude, but in my mind I was thinking that as a grown man, why on earth would they feel the need to check up on me?

I arrived on Grafton Street early at 3.30am. It turns out that staying overnight in a cheap Dublin city centre hostel makes it incredibly easy to arise early. In fact, you hardly sleep at all!

Drunken slurs, wild shouting and doors banging regularly are experienced all night. I stayed in the hostel, as Dublin had no temple in 2001.

I found myself opening out the 'Chanting 100,000 names of God' banner in a dark Mad Max post-apocalyptic world of urban chaos. To a vegetarian who had lived in tranquillity on a remote island, I found myself in a different world. Cow-meat trailer kitchens (they hang up animals by their hind legs and slit their throats); glass being smashed; drunken arguments, and police sirens were experienced all around me. And I had thought no one would be here at this time. So much for me thinking the street would be deserted! A guy stumbled over, read the sign, and glanced at my white robes. In a raw Dublin accent, "Jaysus bud, stor-ree, wha' are you doin' man?"

I smiled at him, "We're doing a chant for peace today… Hare Krishna!"

Things went well. Around 30 people had turned up by midday. At one point it started raining. The cardboard bellows of the keyboard harmonium and the sound equipment don't really get on well in the rain. A devotee from Croatia disappeared and returned 15 minutes later with a shelter-giving gazebo. It was a spontaneous gesture from him and a decent thing to do. The gazebo was gratefully appreciated and made use of for the rest of the day.

***

From the previous year, a group of Hungarian girls in their twenties had been in Ireland distributing books about Krishna consciousness. The Hungarian girls were very impressive. They remained focused, sincere, disciplined, enthusiastic and hard-working. By the 20th Century 'The West' – a loose confederation of North America, Australasia and Western Europe – had climbed to the top of the international socio-political ladder. Their popular culture through the entertainment and fashion industries was internationally dominant. However, lethargy is the curse of the egotistical front-runner. At the top, one starts to relax, slow down, and get comfortable – too comfortable. And before you know it, some of your people are lazy. This can happen in richer countries. And other regions – recently restricted by the former Soviet Union but now free – start catching up.

Was it for this reason or some other? Who knows? But we at Hare Krishna Ireland were far behind the enthusiasm and progress of the Hungarian Society for Krishna Consciousness.

In Ireland our main temple building has looked a little scruffy for most of its life as a temple. The organisation has struggled to really develop the property and the community.

At the Hungarian rural temple, however, they have 200 committed enthusiasts hosting tens of thousands of visitors annually with 200 hectares for farming, and 70 cows and bulls. They have their own school building, an animal hotel for the Holy Cows, two life-sized elephants at the entrance gate (not real living animals, mind you) and a retreat centre for yoga. Under the leadership of Sivarama Swami they have somehow developed a joyful and operational spiritual community that was a favourite poster child for Hare Krishna communities everywhere in the world. I had some experience of the Krishna commune culture; however, the Hungarians were simply all round doing things bigger and better.

"What am I doing with my life?" I began to wonder. Among all the young people I could see; these four girls Pushpa-gopal devi dasi, Nishanta-Lila devi dasi, Ananda devi dasi, and Anuragi devi dasi were more determined, more focused, more pure and more positively connected. "Whatever they have, I want more of," I thought.

Then a letter arrived from Sivarama Swami, dated January 22nd 2003:

'Dear Tim... I am in receipt of your letter dated the 8th and 23rd July and have noted the contents.

I read both your letters and the enclosed poems. I was happy that you decided to remain in Dublin and help Manu. I will not give you too much advice as you repeatedly write that you can accept it in theory only, therefore let me not take too much time, however, I will say this. You are not a scientist, neither will you be one, neither will you be able to do scientific preaching. If you were, you would have done it long ago.

The high point of your devotional career was when you were working under authority at Inish Rath. Until you put yourself in the same situation you will not achieve any devotional results.

Neither can you make it in the material world. Firstly as a devotee you cannot long associate with non-devotee people. Second, you have little karma for making money. Therefore you should decide whether you want to be an independent nobody always striving to be somebody or whether you will be someone's servant. That is my advice.'

End of letter.

Here the word 'servant' is referring to the aspiration to be a servant of God, or to serve others. In bhakti and yoga circles 'service' is the translation of the Sanskrit word **seva** (pronounced 'say'vah'). A devotee is trying to learn to *serve* Krishna, the devotees, and all of humanity.

After several months of contemplation, I decided to return to the lake isle of Inish Rath and abandon the vague idea to use a university education in society, when my destiny lay elsewhere. Inish Rath as a project has challenges with finding its purpose, but then I have challenges with finding purpose myself. I was delighted to be back living by the lakelands in a temple of tranquillity.

Due to the blessings of Srila Prabhupad, the founder of the International Society for Krishna Consciousness, and due to the purity of the ashram residents, one can again easily fit into the regulation of arising between 3.00am and 4.00am daily for prayer and meditation. It's really quite wonderful. And then one naturally wants to share this with others.

We would continue to travel to Dublin's main shopping street every Saturday afternoon to chant and dance. The Hungarian girls would often join us.

One day a man was acting like a buffoon right in front of the chanting party of 10 devotees. He was making snide remarks, frivolous comments and inappropriate gestures. This continued on for 15 minutes, and he was distracting and confusing various onlookers.

I asked him to stop. He continued. I asked him to stop again, and he carried on. I warned him. He couldn't care less. I stood there in pure white robes from head to toe and glared at him. He was the same height as me, and our eyes met directly. Suddenly – like a lightning strike – my head headbutted his head. It just came over me. He stumbled back flabbergasted in indescribable shock. "What the… did ye see wha' he did? Did ye see?" he said with a flat Dublin accent. He stumbled around looking at the crowd on the street pointing at me and rambling again, appealing for sympathy, and acting a little like a bully who had just been slapped. But am I being harsh on him, as I struck first?

The chanting of the mantra helps to make one somewhat fearless. He stumbled over and punched me in the head. I stood my ground. The poor man was still having trouble dealing with the intense surprise, and while I stood motionless he continued to wheel around, rambling, and appealing to the crowd. There and then I was thankful that he punched the side and top of my head, as I don't know what happens if one punches someone with glasses straight in the face. I don't fancy a shard of glass going into my eyes. That thought, among others, actually popped into my mind at that moment.

Just then the two Hungarian girls Nisanta-Lila and Ananda came to my two sides and together, spontaneously and simultaneously, they led me by my arms and brought me away from this man. Then they placed me in a safer position more surrounded by other devotees and our street paraphernalia... mantra board, instruments, book table, etc. It was a decent attempt at trying to avoid the incident escalating further.

It was quite exciting. I had never been in a fight before or since. But I believed the man needed some kind of firm treatment, as he didn't seem interested in polite words. It worked... and moments later this man staggered on up the street mumbling in disbelief, but finally leaving us in peace. Later on that day I talked to Manu about this. He didn't really approve of my actions. I think he thought I was trying to impress the girls, like boys do. He was probably right. Retrospectively, I see that I had mixed motivations. Maybe there could have been a more peaceful way to get the desired result, but sometimes a person with the required abilities and understanding is not present in the moment, so the job gets done in a less perfect way.

As I struck first, someone might rightly question if I was being decent and moral. Within myself, I remember three motivations. (1) A ridiculously boyish attempt to impress the girls. (2) general anger (not spiritual at all) which was born from unfulfilled lust, as explained by Krishna in Bhagavad Gita 3.37. (3) A slightly sincere attempt to find justice and try to teach an out-of-control man some kind of lesson, in the only way I felt could work in this situation. Two of the three reasons listed here are not befitting a monk, so I apologise to the man, and to human society, for my improper behaviour.

Having said that, the traditional Vedic system of managing human society is not lenient on people that require correction. Once, in my parent's house, I watched a TV documentary about thievery on the same shopping street where this incident took place, Grafton Street. Thieves steal from shops, are caught, go to jail for a few days or a few weeks, return to the same shopping street, are eventually caught again, return to prison, stay for a little while, are released, and return to stealing. Some offenders treat prison as a short break from their families and 'work'. They're really not being corrected, are they? A Vedic king would physically punish a repeat offender and, remember, this is within a culture that promotes ahimsa, or non-violence, as a general principal. The offender in this story did a minor offence, but the 'punishment' was fairly minor also. His main reaction was really intense shock, and I think his ego was a little damaged. He did have the opportunity to retaliate and strike me back, which I allowed him to do. The punishment inflicted on the man did also get the desired result. That is, it was effective.

***

Inish Rath Island had gone through a cultural change from the period when I lived there before. As a student monk, it used to be my service to ring a large brass bell at mealtimes, at 8.30am and 1.00pm.

During the '80s and '90s someone would ring this bell, wait, and all the residents would come fairly promptly at the sound. The assembled devotees would then sing a prayer in Sanskrit as a blessing and *grace before meals*. Next, one or two servers would take the sacred food around and dish it out to all present. The culture is that the server keeps serving everyone and cheerfully encourages everyone to eat more of the delicious and holy food. Only when it's clear that everyone else has finished does he eat himself. He is not actually supposed to save any for himself or to think of himself at all. His main focus and interest is to just serve others.

Only if there is some food left over will he eat himself. In practice, it never really happened that the food ran out. However, occasionally there might be only a few hot, mouth-watering temple-made samosas. So the server might end up serving them all out.

This is ashram serving culture - going on in temples since antiquity. However, in the two years I was away in Dublin, all the residents from before, apart from the eternally present Mother Maha-Mantra Devi Dasi, had changed to new people. Somewhere along the way this serving culture had gotten lost. There was now a 21st Century self-service buffet. The holy food was brought out at the mealtimes and residents wandered along in their own time and served themselves. Traditional serving culture still went on as normal on Sunday, but it seemed that the midweek family spirit had become somewhat broken. Not all the time, as now and again someone would have a birthday, and Mother Maha-Mantra baked them a cake, like we were all in a family. But the twice-a-day every day meal culture appeared to have gotten influenced by a degree of modern impersonalism.

In addition to this change, the temple had a new problem to contend with: rats. The abundance of food and water, and the dearth of predators, allowed the rat population to grow with impressive speed. You know things are bad when you can see rats darting around in the middle of the day – going from bush to bush just outside the main building. It got to a stage when many people stopped coming to the temple. The manager, Manu, was mostly away attempting to fund-raise to keep the temple open, so I kept him updated by telephone. As in India, where cows, monkeys, and all manner of animals have the freedom to roam in human population centres, Vedic culture likes to allow life to spread and multiply. But, what do you do with **rats**? They were getting into the building taking food, urinating and leaving droppings. I have heard of a modern-day mystical story from South America where one Hare Krishna swami performed a sacrificial ceremony and asked rats infesting a temple to leave for elsewhere. He communicated to the beasts in a mystical meditation, and apparently they left. But none of us here had a mystical bone in our bodies. Manu took the practical approach and asked me to phone the local county council and request their pest control service to come. So they came... it took four visits to kill all the rats. It was a difficult and unpalatable decision. Although the Veda encourages non-violence (ahimsa) and vegetarianism, the killing of an aggressor is sometimes seen as necessary, especially if this aggressor could kill people under your protection with weapons or disease.

***

I have previously mentioned about the farm community in Hungary, one of the most successful Hare Krishna temples in the world, and one of the most self-sufficient communities by any measure. Under inspiration from Srila Prabhupad, the founder / acarya (spiritual head) of the Society, this particular temple was founded by Sivarama Swami. For day-to-day management, the temple had a Temple President in charge, who was a married man in his thirties at that time. The Hungarian TP's wife was also very active in the development of their community. And then it came to transpire that she actually identified as being homosexual. At that time, in that place, this became a slight scandal, as the place was a model community, so marriage break-up was not seen as being ideal, let alone if it turns out that one of the partner's prefers people of the same sex; let alone if that couple was expected to turn into the 'first family' (to use American presidential terminology).

I think that Sivarama Swami felt this young woman was feeling the pressures of life, so he wanted to send her somewhere where she would be looked after in a temple environment, but she would be far away from any gossip, scandal, and the like. And just to give her time to think. So where to go, but Inish Rath Island? She stayed with us for about two months in the early winter time. I believe this helped to give everyone involved some time to adjust to the new situation.

What is the Hare Krishna view on homosexuality? The reader would really have to talk to each individual to get an answer. I think overall most believers and followers of this religion are respectful of other people's choices and circumstances. I know several devotees, some quite senior, who are gay. They give lectures in temples; however they do not publically talk about their sexual preferences. One Hare Krishna swami conducted a gay marriage ceremony. Some swamis and gurus were agreeable, others were vehemently opposed.

***

In 2003 I was requested to sign up as being a legal director of the Society in Northern Ireland, and later in Ireland. ISKCON NI Ltd had one property in Northern Ireland, namely Inish Rath Island. Similarly, ISKCON Ireland had only one property, 83 Middle Abbey Street, Dublin 1.

If someone looks on paper (or on screen) and sees that I was a director of the charity in the two jurisdictions, it almost looks like I was somewhat in charge. I wasn't. As a voluntary service, I went to meetings, signed a lot of papers, and whoever was managing a property was going ahead and doing whatever they were doing anyway. I would say hardly anyone even knew I was one of the directors. I didn't do very much directing. I think some older members of the Society simply wanted someone who wouldn't give them any hassle, challenges or stress as being a co-director.

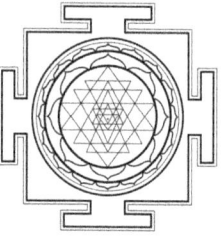

- Bhagavad Gita verse -

- Temple Room – Inish Rath Island -

12

2004:

Machine-Gun Chanting

There was an Indian man from Bengal living on the island, a decent enough man. He was a very expert and dynamic player of the mridanga drum in temple kirtan music. He had come for work. In an effort to keep the temple running, Manu Das began to bring over Indians from the subcontinent. The temple simply couldn't find Irish or English local people to do certain altar rituals and services which are daily events. Private donors shared modest monthly maintenance contributions with people in the temple who were serving in this way. This man was one of the first to come. He was missing his wife and young son. He struggled with the midweek solitude and empty silence as compared with the noise and bustle of family-orientated India. He stayed for three years and then he returned to his family. I had the distinct impression that he would not want to repeat the experience of living on a remote island, by a still silent lake, with not a soul in sight on a Monday morning in November or a Tuesday afternoon in February, or any other of these cold quiet days.

Another man who came from far away was called MM. He seemed very helpful. Manu had obtained a loan of £20,000 and some rooms were being converted into *en suite* guest bedrooms by Derek and Nagnajiti (who lived on the mainland just across from the island) so MM was helping in the kitchen, on the altar, and with the construction work. However, something terrible was to transpire.

Allegations were made that this man was touching young children inappropriately. A parent involved at the time told me that she was aware of five families who made statements. It was a shock for everyone. Nothing like this happened around here: this was a safe haven, a place to get away from a harsh, cruel world, and MM had *seemed so nice*.

As I was a young single man, I had no business interacting with children, so some details were told to me by others. While MM was visiting another part of the country on some service for the temple, later a parent from that place contacted the temple to lodge these serious complaints.

After this, other young children came forward. Kids would visit on Sundays with their parents, and hang out in the play area which was situated by mature woodlands. These tall old trees formed a protective band around the lake island. Children began to report that MM had touched them also. After some time an angry parent phoned the police, and later management was criticised for procrastinating.

One parent had to really restrain himself from pummelling MM into the ground. I personally saw the struggle in his face as he tried to restrain himself. Some parents spent hours in the local police station, as the children were very sensitively questioned. The authorities concluded there was not enough physical evidence to prosecute, but the individual was held for some time, and then deported. A social worker mentioned to a parent that paedophiles can sometimes seek out groups that provide access to children. As the island is such a safe space, it has the potential to attract these types of people, as they hope children and families might let their guards down.

***

Another group of four girls – this time from New Zealand – were travelling and sharing the culture and philosophy of Krishna consciousness, and they passed through the temple. Whoops... one of the girls was Grace who had received a handwritten letter expressing love from me more than five years earlier. Awkward.

I noticed that Grace was quite tall. With eyes smeared with the balm of love in my even younger youth, I hadn't noticed her height years ago. Being not so tall myself, my statistical chances to match with a medium-tall girl were slim. When they were going back to Dublin before returning to England I suggested we all go to Grafton Street to chant for the benefit of the general public. One of the girls was a wonderful singer, and they could all dance like gopis (angels). There was another girl from the Czech Republic who had a concert violin. We chanted and danced – or the girls danced – for several hours and it was a beautiful spectacle. Large crowds on the pedestrian street would stop to experience the exotic sari-clad 20-something-year-old girls twirling in time, as they sang Hare Krishna accompanied by the culturally enriching and tastefully amplified violin.

By evening we were all tired, hungry and happy. I acquired all the food remaining unsold in Govinda's Restaurant and we had a feast that tasted like cuisine of the spiritual world that evening. In a moment aside I had a chance to politely apologise again to Grace for my previous boyishness. All in all, it was a very good day.

***

Zac was an English man in his early thirties with a cockney accent. He was an aspirational wheeler-dealer of the Only Fools and Horses variety, who came to live on the island for over a year. Some of the men loaned him money, and they never got it back. But deep down he had a good heart. He gave the impression of being the type of person who had made use of the generous welfare system found in Northern Europe. He tended to exaggerate. He knew a little Tai Chi and Qi-gong. A large photo of him appeared in the local county newspaper holding his hands in an Oriental-looking Chi pose with the caption 'Zac, Head of the Dragon Palms Institute of Tai Chi, now based at Hare Krishna Island'. That's what he had told some reporter. It gave a few of us some giggles. Had he ever even *worked* before, let alone been the **'Head of an Institute'**?!

I don't mean to criticise. He had a subtle decency, kind of like he was honest in his streetwise dishonesty. To be fair, he actually showed me some Qi Gong, and I frequently share this with others to this day. I use this as part of a forest meditation and when practising mindfulness in a woodland setting.

✳✳✳

Somehow I got to hear that BBC Ulster Radio was promoting music events. On a certain day an organisation could host a musical event, and the venues and times would all get free radio advertising.

"Music," I thought, "We're into music… we sing and chant all day."

A chair for sitting down was a kind of luxury in the temple back then, but Manu Das had purchased 58 green plastic chairs for the general public. I registered a sacred chant concert with the radio station, and then I unearthed some old Hare Krishna festival posters with a beautiful picture of child Krishna that former Head Monk Tribhuvanatha Das had used.

With visits to a cyber cafe, photocopying, and cutting and gluing pieces of paper, I re-used old posters and then made some simple leaflets. Then I went around the local villages putting up posters and popping leaflets into the letterboxes of our countryside neighbours in Teemore, Derrylin and Lisnaskea.

On the concert day, we stuck together two tables and covered them with a large exotic cotton sheet from India to make a 'stage'. I invited Praghosa Das to come from Dublin to be the MC and there were seven devotees with short slots of 15 minutes chanting and singing, with a mid-event interval: the whole experience was to last two hours. But would anyone come? I drove the temple ferryboat to the mainland and waited… and waited… the summer evening event was to be for two hours and there I was standing alone in a still, lakeside car park at 6.22pm with not a soul in sight for the 6.30pm first ferry.

My ears strained for the encouraging sound of a car engine and I waited. Irish people are not noted for their punctuality. A car came, and then another, and two more together, then a van. More people were emerging from the vehicles, as suddenly crowds were forming. Locals were chatting and there was a buzz in the air. The event went really, really well. People came, listened, clapped their hands, and tapped their feet. The temple was jam-packed. All 58 chairs were occupied, so the Hare Krishna people ended up sitting on the floor, which they were used to doing anyway. There was a feeling of satisfaction and joy in the atmosphere.

When everyone had left, I wandered slowly around the island chanting japa, murmuring the Hare Krishna mantra on wooden beads. I experienced the most focused, mindful, attentive, peaceful and blissful quiet mantras I have ever repeated in my life. I was pacing slowly through the woodland path and the holy names were rolling off my tongue easily and beautifully. Distraction, clutter, laziness and disinterest were strikingly non-present; and instead, I had an intense experience of being given mercy.

It's an unusual analogy, but this is how it felt. Just as a machine gun is firing out bullets, similarly the holy names were shooting out from my mouth and destroying anything negative and unfortunate, leaving beauty and calm. As the bullets of a machine gun are numerous, lethal and effective; similarly each of the many mantras flowing out was effective and focused, destroying all misfortune.

It was the happiest day of my life. I had had the honour of serving both the mission of the temple, and other people, of my own free-will. It was satisfying.

Before the event, Manu didn't think any local people would come, and Praghosa from Dublin had asked for the proceeds of the event. About £600 was collected in donations and ticket sales on the evening. This money ended up being contributed to victims of child abuse in Hare Krishna temples. Several months before, some people in the USA had sued the Society as they had been abused as children. If I recall correctly, the amount was for several hundred million dollars. As most of the schools were either in the USA or India, temples in those countries had to pay most of the money. However, all temples internationally were requested to make a contribution.

In describing my feelings at the end of this concert, I described it as the happiest day in my life. That was describing my personal feelings on that day in connection with sharing the mantra, separately from how I see and relate to disgraceful child abuse. Unfortunately, practically any organisation in this world can be infiltrated by people who lie, cheat and cause pain to others. Religions can be soft targets for these evil people, as religionists are often idealistic and also apparently very outwardly forgiving. Accordingly, some people *act* like they are good, and try to find space or openings to get into the company of god-brothers and god-sisters.

***

A couple of months later Sivarama Swami visited the island and Praghosa Das joyfully related the concert highlights to him. I saw swami's face light up and sparkle hearing about it, as sharing the mantra with new people in a positive way is part of the essence of a temple.

- Peacock on Inish Rath Island -

- Upper L. Erne, County Fermanagh -

Epilogue

I had the fortune of having an ashram experience for 12 years, including the time when I was 17 going on 18 and the temple experience became an integral part of my life. I had started to skip college lectures and could hardly wait for the course to be finished so I could move in with the monks.

For two of these 12 years, I was back in the city, attending university again, but during this time I was very much in ashram consciousness. I still arose early to chant 'rounds' on wooden beads, and I both attended and arranged many functions to do with kirtan chanting or Vedic philosophy. In total, I lived in the temple ashram for nine and a half years, seven of which I was wearing the saffron robes of a monk.

Finally, at the start of 2005, I moved out and started to put my mind towards work and paying bills, but I had had such an experience during my youth that I found I had to work to make an income using what I learned in the temple. I set up my own business in the hospitality and mind-body-spirit industry. Initially, business was very slow. For the first few years my income was less than what it would have been on social welfare, but gradually things picked up. Now I'm a happily married man with three children.

In my case, I had a positive experience living in an ashram. Not everyone is so lucky. In the history of religious institutions and organisations – the International Society for Krishna Consciousness included – some people have had to experience misogyny, racism, sexual abuse, financial ruin and psychological torture from deceitful leaders, showy preachers, or manipulative managers. In contrast, real religion is summarised in Srimad Bhagavatam 1.2.6.

The supreme occupation [dharma] for all humanity is that by which every soul can attain to loving devotional service unto the transcendent Lord. Such devotional service must be unmotivated and uninterrupted to completely satisfy the Self.

***

During the years I lived as a brahmachari student monk I never for a moment expected I would continue living in this way all my life. I was aware it was a training period. I did come across people passing through the ashram who had experienced frustrations or challenges in their lives. Maybe things didn't work out in some relationship, and then they would make statements denigrating marriage, saying that they will be a full-time monk or temple devotee for the rest of their lives.

Sometimes the universe is trying to teach us something about ourselves, and we stubbornly refuse to listen. But even a person in a happy relationship can be mindful that this too is a stage. There will be a time when we are forced to separate from our partner (at death). Part of the ashram experience is that we get to know ourselves as an individual. Bhagavad Gita Chapter 2 Verse 12 hints that the one thing that we will always have is our individuality. As an individual, we can choose to see spirit everywhere, if we so desire.

***

Who am I? Many of us on a spiritual search are wondering this. Where did I come from? Before she married Dad, my mother had been married before. My *biological* father, throughout his life, had a fairly severe psychological challenge with schizophrenia. In 1973 when my mother began dating her first husband, initially she wasn't fully aware of his mental health problems. Later, for my physical and emotional safety, she left him. She genuinely felt Baby Tim was in danger with a man who wasn't in control of himself. She returned to him, trying her best to do the right thing, and my brother Alan was born, but when I was age four she felt again that her husband, without even being fully aware of this himself, posed a serious threat to two little boys. She took us back to the family home and our Aunt Frances. Two years later, through a mutual friend, she met our Dad, Brian. Although Ireland had no divorce until 1997, fortunately for us the Roman Catholic Church would grant marriage annulments in extreme situations, so the marriage was dissolved.

The day I was born my mother recounts that I initially struggled to breathe and to live. So I was protected for a week in an incubator, all the while being attended to by doctors and nurses. During that time, while my mother was still in the hospital herself, my biological father went to the name registration office and quietly intimidated an old lady behind the desk to register my name as Mortimer Hall. An uncle later joked that was like a name of a 19th century English lord. This was the name I was told as a boy. In my late forties I discovered that the name written into the initial birth certificate was Mortimeor (sic) Peacock Hall. This is like a name not just given to an English aristocrat, but to a flamboyant playboy lord of the 18th or 19th centuries who lives life extravagantly, lavishly spending his family's ancestral fortune. My poor mother got the shock of her life when she was released from hospital and she went to register my name. When she tried to have the name changed, she was told by officials that it was too late – the name had gone through and had been authenticated. My family never used that name, of course… but a syllable of it, the 'Tim' bit – became my name.

I met Dad in 1981. He gave me some much needed male guidance. When my mother and father began dating, initially she would tell little Tim and Alan that this nice man coming to collect her (for dates) was a taxi driver!

Throughout my boyhood I had this background feeling of trying to discover myself emotionally. Although Dad and I exchange hugs now, during my youth he too was trying to discover how he fit into this situation. We formed our family in an unconventional way, and it took each of us a little time to find our place. These would all have been motivating factors that inspired me to move into the temple ashram: a search for finding myself on many levels. We soulfully crave love, acceptance and our place in the world.

My biological father lived in mental health care homes managed by the State for the remainder of his life (until he died in 2020). My mother was his most frequent visitor. She shed the most tears his funeral. (I was honoured to be able to sing the Hare Krishna mantra at this funeral.) With her new husband, our Dad, we never used the term 'stepfather'. I think my parents were very emotionally mature to work through all of this.

***

In one sense, our names are temporary designations given to us by others. In 1975 a little old lady was strongly persuaded to register a certain name in a registry office. Years later, in a solicitor's office, I was officially registered by deed poll as 'Tim McEvitt'. The surname 'Hall' is an English name. The name 'McEvitt' is an Irish name. Is my origin here, or there? Most people in America, for example, trace their roots back to various places in Europe. We all have this search for 'origins'. There was a time when the island of Ireland was attached to the European mainland. Was it called 'Ireland' then? No. The physical appearance and name of the 300-mile-long island changes over thousands and millions of years. *Things* move and undergo transformational changes in time.

The spiritual search is a search to discover ourselves as an individual being; independent of where we find ourselves, and what other people call us. The spiritual search is a search to discover sat-cid-ananda; that is, eternality, wisdom and inner happiness. The ancient text Bhagavad Gita discusses these issues; however it takes time to understand.

Bhagavad Gita 7.8

Krishna says:
I am the taste of water,
The light of the sun and the moon,
The syllable Om in the Vedic mantras;
I am the sound in ether
And ability in man.

This book is dedicated to my parents, Brian and Noeleen McEvitt and my teachers Sivarama Swami and Tribhuvanatha Das. Thank you. Hare Krishna.

Addendum

> I asked my mother to say something about *her* experience of me joining the temple, so she sent me this.
>
> By Noeleen McEvitt...

I wasn't a bit pleased when you told me you were joining the Hare Krishnas. They had a temple in Dame Street and I worked in an office job on this same street at that time. I worked on the first floor and sometimes I would look out the window and see Hare Krishna people passing by. I thought, "That's all I need: to look out my office window and see my son dancing up the street. Jesus, the embarrassment!" One of my colleagues was an awful jeer and I dreaded the comments from him particularly.

I made it my business to find out more about these Hare Krishnas as I was afraid they were all on drugs and I didn't want them to drag my son down with them. Brian and I made an appointment to see a man who was considered an expert on the various religious cults which were around at the time. His name was Mike Garde, a South African-born theologian and Mennonite. He had an office in Abbey Street over the Veritas shop which sold religious articles and books. He went through the various religious cults with us and assured us that the Hare Krishnas were NOT a cult. They were just a different religion and had been very successful in getting young people OFF drugs. They were just high on life, not drugs. He explained to us that it was an Eastern-based religion believing in one God, just like we as Catholics believe in one God. However, instead of following the teachings of Jesus, they didn't believe that Jesus was part of a Trinity and had a different belief system. Different, but not bad. He said that, unlike certain other so-called religions, there was nothing sinister about Hare Krishna.

When I examined my own belief system I had to admit that we were really à *la carte* Catholics, so why was I getting myself all riled up because my son had decided to follow a different path? Truth be told, our 'belief' was actually very shaky, and getting shakier by the day with all the scandals in the Church that were emerging.

After our visit to Mike Garde, I visited the man who was the current temple president in Dame Street and had a long chat with him. I came away from that meeting with the feeling that the Hare Krishna ideology was not unlike the Catholic Church 50 years before, with a restrictive and high-minded way of life: no alcohol, no sex outside marriage, no drugs. He spoke about the restrictive sex rule in a very open way which I appreciated having lived through a culture that was less than open about that subject. The big sin in Ireland was sex, and the way the subject was treated led to all sorts of abuses and cover ups. One of the things the Hare Krishna president told me was that the orange robes signified that the person wearing these robes was a celibate monk and this designation was taken seriously. If at any time the celibate monk was having difficulties with the celibacy issue they talked it out, and if that state was problematic for the monk then they might decide to change their status and perhaps get married. This way of thinking nearly blew my mind away. I felt this was a much healthier way of thinking than the Catholic Church way where supposedly celibate priests had to remain a priest for life. The evidence was there that this particular system and lifestyle was cluttered with abuses like alcoholic priests and child abuse.

The temple in Dame Street became for me a little oasis in the middle of my working day. I started going at lunch time and had delicious vegetarian food served to me a few times a week. I met another lady there who worked in a bank on Dame

Street and she and I enjoyed the food while sitting on the floor and laughing together at the idea of what our colleagues would say if they could see us!

After you went to live permanently on Inish Rath Island I spent a weekend there and enjoyed the physical labour of gardening and hay-cutting with Aniruddha (Andy). I never involved myself in the religious aspect of the Movement - I just went there for a quiet weekend. However, I do remember on one occasion being very overwhelmed by an intensely emotional response that I had while in the temple and listening to the singing. I was so overwhelmed that I had to leave the room and couldn't stop crying, for what I didn't know. Just pure emotion. One of the women said she had seen that happen before.

Thanks, Photo Descriptions and Credits

Thank you to everyone who gave feedback and suggestions when preparing this book, especially Barbara McLoughlin, Grainne Sullivan, Deirdre Kennedy, Emmett Mullaney, Alex Todd, Eleanor McClean and Joanne O'Brien..

Thank you to the hundreds of volunteers who have helped maintain the Inish Rath Island temple over the decades.

Front Cover	Misty island with rowing boat	Tim McEvitt
Back Cover	Tim at age 21	Shyamananda Das
Chapter 1	Reading Srimad Bhagavatam	Jagannatha Suta Das
Chapter 1	Shyamananda (early 20s) and Tim (teen)	Rachel Fitzgerald
Chapter 2	Radhadesh Temple in Belgium	Temple Admin
Chapter 2	Sharma Das on book distribution	Mick Duff
Chapter 3	Inish Rath Island	Dean
Chapter 3	A monk in silent meditation	Stephen Barnes
Chapter 4	Children in India	Mick Duff
Chapter 4	An ox at Krishna Valley, Hungary	Tim McEvitt

Chapter 5	Temple Altar – Inish Rath Island	Dina Tarini Devi Dasi
Chapter 5	Young monks in Dublin temple, 1997	Mick Duff
Chapter 6	Inish Rath House	Tim McEvitt
Chapter 6	Janaki	Jaganntha Suta Das
Chapter 7	Special morning on the lake	Tim McEvitt
Chapter 7	Shyamananda and a young deer	Tim McEvitt
Chapter 8	Painting of Krishna as a boy	BBT Publishers, used with permission
Chapter 8	Janaki and beads	Jagannatha Suta Das
Chapter 9	Temple Room	Stephen Barnes
Chapter 9	Tribhuvanatha Das	Festival team
Chapter 10	Kirtan chanting on the streets of Dublin	Harinam Ruci
Chapter 10	Kirtan in Dublin temple	Akhandadhi Das
Chapter 11	Inish Rath Island – aerial view	Jagannatha Suta Das
Chapter 11	Forest walk on Inish Rath	Tim McEvitt
Chapter 12	Bhagavad Gita verse	Martina Kenji
Chapter 12	Temple Room – Inish Rath Island	Tim McEvitt
End	Peacock on Inish Rath Island	Shyamananda Das
End	Upper L. Erne, County Fermanagh	Malachy O'Connor

List of Well-known Sanskrit Words

For a history of Sanskrit as compared with the contemporary language theory referred to as 'Proto-Indo European', please see Devamrita Swami's book, Searching for Vedic India. Sanskrit is the language of the ancient texts of the Veda.

Avatar	One who descends into a body
Ayurveda	Ancient nature-based holistic health system
Aryan	Noble people. Borrowed and redefined by Hitler in the 1930s and 1940s.
Buddha	An enlightened being
Chakra	An energy centre in the body
Deva	A godly being, seen in words like 'Divine'.
Guru	A teacher
Govinda	A name of Krishna
Hare Krishna	First two names of a well-known mantra
Karma	Reaction to our work or choices
Kama-Sutra	A famous text on eroticism
Mantra	A sacred sound vibration
Mandala	A circular symmetrical design
Mahatma	A great soul
Nirvana	A state of enlightenment

Om	The universal sound that conveys omniscience and omnipotence
Pura and Puri	City, seen in names like Canter**bury**, **borough**, Edin**burgh**, Singa**pore**
Raj	Raja – a king
Samsara	The cycle of birth and death
Swami	A renounced monk
Sant	A holy person or saint, seen in 'Santa Claus', and 'saint'
Swastika	Ancient energy symbol, borrowed by the Nazis
Tantra	A type of instructional text
Yoga	Connection between the individual self and the greater universe
Zen	This is a Japanese word that comes from the Sanskrit 'dhyana'

Appendix

Sankirtan

Canto 6, Chapter 3, Verse 32 of the Srimad Bhagavatam states, with Saint Sukadeva Goswami talking to a powerful ruler:

"My dear King, the chanting of the holy name of the Lord is able to uproot even the reactions of the greatest sins. Therefore, the chanting of the sankirtan movement is the most auspicious activity in the entire universe. Please try to understand this so that others will take it seriously".

San-kirtan (sankirtan) is the chanting of holy names for the benefit of everyone everywhere. If the reader doesn't connect with the word 'sin' mentioned above, after centuries of verbal abuse from certain quarters, then it is a question of whether we're talking about the desire to enjoy or control things beyond what is our natural birthright, or which cause suffering to others. The Vedic understanding is that when we do these things, we create bad karma, which acts like suffocating weeds smothering the true nature of the soul. Joyful singing of powerful mantras uproots these weeds. Mantras are Holy Names. We're asking for help.

The SB verse quoted contains two significant claims. Firstly, the chanting of the holy names of God is able to remove karma from the individual. These are reactions to the actions that we perform that negatively affect others. Secondly, chanting and singing the names of God is the most auspicious activity in the entire universe.

***

Some people might think, "Aha… just another religion making a bold claim that no one really knows, and no one can substantiate." However, **we** don't know what everyone does or doesn't know; and perhaps these statements can be investigated and maturely contemplated over time. If one studies all 18,000 verses of the SB, and participates in 100 hours of sankirtan in various locations around the world, one would be in a better position to understand these claims. And why not? How many hours of work and research do people take to complete a Masters Degree or a PhD? One might be working on a PhD maybe to add something to human society, but a large part of the motivation for many people is to get a job, which boils down to food, shelter, protecting one's dependents, and a comfortable place to sleep. But every Tom, Dick and Harry mammal or bird out there is doing the same thing. So, before we reject the bold statements completely, one idea is to make a serious investigation into it. I pray the reader will bless me so that I take these meditations seriously.

***

If you would like to listen to lectures of our Head Monk Tribhuvanatha Das one can download multiple lectures at no cost from audio.iskcondesiretree.com. Click on 'ISKCON Prabhujis'; then choose 'ISKCON Prabhujis S-Y'. Scroll down to 'Tribhuvanatha Prabhu'. You can find his lectures and recorded music sessions here.

***

To experience Kirtan in a present-day concert setting, please attend a Radhika Das concert.

*Available worldwide from Amazon
and all good bookstores*

www.mtp.agency

mtp.agency

@mtp_agency